READING, PRAYING, LIVING
POPE FRANCIS'S REJOICE AND BE GLAD

Reading, Praying, Living Pope Francis's Rejoice and Be Glad

A Faith Formation Guide

Daniel P. Horan, OFM

LITURGICAL PRESS

Collegeville, Minnesota

www.litpress.org

© 2019 by Daniel P. Horan, OFM
Published by Liturgical Press, Collegeville, Minnesota. All rights reserved. No part of this book may be used or reproduced in any manner whatsoever, except brief quotations in reviews, without written permission of Liturgical Press, Saint John's Abbey, PO Box 7500, Collegeville, MN 56321-7500. Printed in the United States of America.

1   2   3   4   5   6   7   8   9

Library of Congress Cataloging-in-Publication Data

Names: Horan, Daniel P., author.
Title: Reading, praying, living Pope Francis's Rejoice and be glad : a faith
    formation guide / Daniel P. Horan, OFM.
Description: Collegeville, Minnesota : Liturgical Press, 2019. | Includes
    bibliographical references.
Identifiers: LCCN 2018035828 | ISBN 9780814664070 (pbk.)
Subjects: LCSH: Catholic Church. Pope (2013– : Francis). Gaudete
    et exsultate. | Holiness—Catholic Church. | Perfection—Religious
    aspects—Catholic Church. | Christian life—Catholic authors. | Catholic
    Church—Doctrines.
Classification: LCC BX2350.5.C383 H67 2019 | DDC 248.4/82—dc23
LC record available at https://lccn.loc.gov/2018035828

Contents

Introduction

There is a striking anecdote about holiness that Thomas Merton, the late American Trappist monk and author, recounts in his 1948 best-selling spiritual autobiography *The Seven Storey Mountain*. He tells of walking down Sixth Avenue in New York City with his friend Robert Lax, the Jewish poet. Merton recalls that at some point Lax turned to him and asked: "What do you want to be, anyway?" Having recently converted to Catholicism, Merton responded: "I don't know; I guess what I want is to be a good Catholic." Without missing a beat, his friend replied: "What do you mean, you want to be a good Catholic? What you should say is that you want to be a saint." Protesting that such a seemingly audacious claim was beyond him, was too difficult, was impossible, he asked Lax how exactly he was to become a saint. "By wanting to," Lax responded. "All that is necessary to be a saint is to want to be one. Don't you believe that God will make you what He created you to be, if you will consent to let Him do it? All you have to do is desire it."[1]

Too often we are like Merton walking down the sidewalk in New York. Whether through the voice of a close friend or a thought in our prayer or a passage in Scripture or a random song lyric, we are invited to consider our call as Christian women and men to live a life of holiness, to become the saints we were created to be. And in response, we frequently dismiss the idea out of hand. Sanctity is for the special, elite, and religious of the church, we might protest, not an ordinary person like me.

But as Christians each of us is, in fact, called to holiness by virtue of our baptism and the gospel life we have promised to live. Holiness should not be equated with external signs of piety or a regimen of private devotions. Holiness is far more inclusive and particular than we like to imagine. When we think it is reserved for some kind of divinely cast group of religious elites, we can too easily exempt ourselves from discerning, embracing, and living out our respective vocations as Christians in whatever time and place we find ourselves. Merton's contemporary and friend, Dorothy Day, the cofounder of the Catholic Worker movement, is attributed with saying often: "Don't call me a saint. I don't want to be dismissed that easily."[2] This was her way of pointing out that most Christians do not take the examples of the saints seriously enough. Sure, we admire the saints from afar; we build our statues, pray our prayers (especially when we lose our keys or need some help), and know the outlines of their heroic lives. But Day's point is that we don't really think their lives and the choices that shaped their lives have anything to do with us *personally*. We might imagine that the canonical saints the church celebrates throughout the liturgical year must have received some kind of special grace, some sort of Christian superpower that allowed them to be so holy. But Day and Lax and so many others want to remind us that saints were just like you and me! They weren't born saints, they were sinners as much as they were saints, but their *desire* to be holy—to do the will of God—is what prevailed. Their choice is also our choice.

But it's a choice we have to make ourselves each and every day. Fortunately, we have a great "cloud of witnesses" (Heb 12:1) to encourage us along the way. And alongside Lax, Merton, and Day, we can add a contemporary voice who speaks with authority and offers us wisdom about how to live the Gospel today: Pope Francis.

> Holiness is far more inclusive and particular than we like to imagine.

Pope Francis has continued to surprise and inspire the church with his actions, preaching, and teaching. Each of these dimensions of his ministry as Bishop of Rome is important and plays a significant role in shaping the life of the church because the pope has a unique responsibility in serving not only the local church of Rome but also the universal church across the globe. This guide is designed to help readers approach, understand, and engage with one of Pope Francis's recent teachings, his apostolic exhortation *Gaudete et Exsultate*—Rejoice and Be Glad—on the universal call to holiness in the modern world. But before we dive into the text itself, it might be worthwhile to situate it within the broader context of church teaching.

Some Catholic Christians are surprised to learn that not all church teachings are of equal weight or significance.[3] There is what the Second Vatican Council—the gathering of the world's bishops in Rome from 1962 to 1965 to address pastoral and doctrinal issues in communion with the pope—calls the "hierarchy of truths." In its Decree on Ecumenism, *Unitatis Redintegratio*, the council fathers made it clear that, "When comparing doctrines with one another, [Christians] should remember that in catholic doctrine there exists an order or 'hierarchy' of truths, since they vary in their relation to the foundation of the Christian faith" (no. 11).[4] Intuitively, this teaching about church teaching makes a lot of sense. Clearly the church's teaching on economic justice or artificial birth control is not of the same weight or importance as, for example, its teaching on the divinity of the Holy Spirit. This ordering or hierarchy is important for us to note because understanding where Pope Francis's latest teaching on holiness fits within the broader deposit of faith will help provide us with additional context.

Most of the teaching authority exercised by the pope is done according to what is technically called "ordinary magisterium." The term "magisterium," while often conflated with the particular bishop or group of bishops doing the teaching, actually refers simply to the teaching authority of the church, which is *exercised* by a bishop or group of bishops in several contexts. Very rarely over the church's two-millennia-long history has this teaching authority—*magisterium*—been exercised in an extraordinary way, which would mean that a particular teaching was taught with the charism of infallibility (i.e., taught irreversibly and without possibility of error concerning our salvation). Typically, the teaching of a pope, exercising ordinary magisterium as universal shepherd and teacher, falls into the levels of teaching commonly known as "authoritative doctrine" or "prudential admonitions." Authoritative doctrine is where, for example, we find many moral teachings of the church. These are not taught with the charism of infallibility but are nonetheless to be taken seriously and assented to by the faithful. Prudential admonitions is a broad category into which numerous teachings can be located, each of which falls short of authoritative doctrine. It is in this last category that we commonly find what theologian Richard Gaillardetz calls "concrete applications of church teaching."[5]

Pope Francis's *Gaudete et Exsultate* (hereafter GE) is precisely a concrete application of church teaching. Specifically, it is, as the pope himself states, an effort "to repropose the call to holiness in a practical way for our own time, with all its risks, challenges and opportunities" (GE 2). Rather than introduce a new doctrine or moral teaching, Pope Francis took the opportunity to address the universal church on the theme of holiness in an effort to develop something previously taught by the Second Vatican Council in its Dogmatic Constitution on the Church, *Lumen Gentium*.

There are a few key themes worth keeping in mind as you read through the apostolic exhortation and move through this guide, themes that will surface over and over again.

1. *Holiness is a universal call rooted in baptism.* The pursuit of holiness is not an optional element of Christian faith,

reserved as it were for a few special people in each generation. Instead, all women and men are called to live a life of Christian discipleship according to the pattern laid out by Jesus in the Gospel and in the contexts in which they find themselves. As Thomas Merton learned from his wise friend, Robert Lax, we are all called to be saints because we are all called to be holy—the question is whether or not we are willing.

2. *Holiness is a communal mission.* There is no such thing as an "independent contractor" or "sole proprietor" or "freelance" Christian. You can only be a Christian in community, which is seen from the very outset of Jesus's life and ministry. Through baptism we are united in the Spirit, and God intends us to support one another in our journey toward Christian holiness. Likewise, just as we can build one another up, we can—and, sadly, often do—become obstacles for one another. Part of what it means to be holy is an increased awareness of the communal dimension of our Christian life.

3. *There are false forms of holiness that threaten to distract us from true holiness.* Pope Francis dedicated two of the five chapters in this exhortation to addressing the threats and challenges we face in striving toward holiness in the modern world. Some of the threats are perennial—various heresies, the temptations of the devil—while others are particularly modern. We must be mindful that the appearance of what some presume is "holy" may not reflect authentic Christian holiness but instead reflect a self-righteous or superficial attitude.

4. *Scripture is the grounding source for Christian holiness.* In responding to the persistent threats of gnosticism in the

second chapter, Pope Francis joins a long Christian tradition of defending the straightforwardness and simplicity of God's revelation to humanity. There is no "secret knowledge" (*gnosis*); nor is there any advanced information that only the saints have access to and that is hidden from us ordinary Christians. The teachings of Jesus are as they appear and, as the pope reiterates throughout this and other texts, are too often "complicated" by Christians who wish to domesticate or water down the Gospel. In addition to referencing the Bible throughout, Pope Francis dedicates his longest chapter to a rich exploration of the Beatitudes in order to show how Scripture is the grounding source for holiness.

5. *Holiness is impossible without prayer.* While this last theme may not have a whole chapter dedicated to it or seem at first glance as prominent as some of the other themes, it is nevertheless present throughout and beneath the whole exhortation. Pope Francis consistently reminds us to call on the Holy Spirit, to seek the intercession of the saints who have gone before us, and to move beyond simply saying prayers toward allowing our whole lives to become a prayer. Furthermore, the pope sees prayer—personal and communal—as the only viable response to the threats Christians face in their journey toward holiness.

Gaudete et Exsultate is an accessible, inspiring, and timely document that is sure to become a classic in Christian spirituality. Pope Francis's reminder about who we claim to be as Christians calls us out of a superficial and complacent way of life and into an exciting and robust life of discipleship and Christian faith. May this guide provide you with a worthwhile resource to understand, reflect, and incorporate this teaching into your own life.

What Holiness Is and Is Not

The first two chapters of *Gaudete et Exsultate* focus on the meaning of holiness, specifically, what it is and what it is not. In chapter 1, Pope Francis begins with restating the tradition we have of holding up Christian women and men who have lived exemplary lives of holiness as role models for contemporary believers. While these capital-*S* Saints are indeed to be celebrated and looked to for guidance, inspiration, and intercession, they are not the only people we can look to for examples of good Christian witness. Pope Francis introduces the notion of "the saints 'next door'" as a way to describe the everyday, ordinary, holy people who may never receive the universal recognition of sainthood but are a kind of saint no less. This is tied to the pope's point that holiness is not something for a few, select, and elite members of the church, but, as the Second Vatican Council teaches, holiness is a universal call for all the baptized. What this call means for us, and how we are called to live in response to that call, is the aim of this chapter.

Chapter 2 takes the complementary perspective: if the meaning of holiness is unpacked in the first chapter, the second one looks at what holiness is not. Pope Francis describes this as "false forms of holiness," and he introduces two ancient heresies that continue to appear in our own age under a new guise: gnosticism and pelagianism. The pope sees these as threats to authentic holiness, which need to be recognized and addressed in our own time, especially in a digital age.

1 The Call to Holiness

Children raised in the Christian faith often learn the stories of the saints early on. The narratives about these holy women and men are usually extraordinary, with the most miraculous or heroic episodes highlighted. As we grow older, it is commonplace for us to retain a certain admiration for these Christian exemplars without ever asking deeper questions about what exactly makes them holy or how their stories are meant to inform our own experience of the faith. Even those who are active churchgoers can remain locked in a well-meaning but superficial appreciation for what it means to be holy, placing the saints in a category removed and distant from the everyday experiences of reality that we encounter.

Recognizing this widespread tendency, Pope Francis opens chapter 1 with a deep dive into what holiness means, who is called to it, and how we might get there. He begins by reiterating what exactly a "saint" is, explaining that the canonical saints (meaning those women and men whose Christian life is officially recognized as a fitting model of Christian discipleship for the universal church) include not only Christians like St. Mary Magdalene or St. Anthony of Padua but also those ancestors of ours in faith that go back to the Hebrew Bible—the great prophets and leaders of the Old Testament such as Sarah and Abraham

(GE 3). All those we hold up as models of how to live God's will in the world constitute what the Letter to the Hebrews describes as "that great cloud of witnesses" or what theologians like Elizabeth Johnson and Benedict XVI have called the "friends of God."[1] Pope Francis reminds us that these great friends of God and prophets are not merely the subjects of fairy tales or inspiring stories to recount from a distance, remembering them as we might recall the characters and plots of our favorite novels. No, these women and men are joined to us in the Holy Spirit according to what we call the communion of saints. "The saints now in God's presence preserve their bonds of love and communion with us" (GE 4), the Holy Father recounts; they are in relationship with us through prayer and the grace of God, and they can assist us through their intercession.

> These women and men are joined to us in the Holy Spirit according to what we call the communion of saints.

What makes these women and men special is not something that comes from without, as in a superpower that God gives to them alone. Instead, it is their ability to respond with a yes to God like that of Mary of Nazareth when she responded to Gabriel's invitation in Luke's gospel: "May it be done to me according to your word" (1:38). To say in an official way that someone is a saint simply means that they followed in Christ's footsteps, imitated the Lord in their unique circumstances and social locations, and offered their lives to God. Sometimes those circumstances mean making the greatest sacrifice for one's faith. "The processes of beatification and canonization recognize the signs of heroic virtue, the sacrifice of one's life in martyrdom, and certain cases where a life is constantly offered for others, even until death" (GE 5).

Pope Francis uses the example of Blessed Maria Gabriella Sagheddu to illustrate this point. To many people, the story of Blessed Maria is an obscure one. She was a young woman born in 1914 in what is now Italy. Most accounts of her early life generally suggest that it was uneventful, even boring. Over time she desired to deepen her faith and eventually entered a Trappist convent as a young woman, where she remained until her death at the young age of twenty-five. What was so eventful about her life? What was so heroic? In brief: nothing. She was someone who in little ways dedicated her life to prayer and reflection, praying in particular for the unity of all Christians. She did this in small yet meaningful ways each day, without fanfare or overt self-interest. Her holiness is seen not in a tremendous singular act, but in the day-to-day decisions she made to follow Christ more closely in all that she did.

As inspiring as the lives of the canonical saints are, we must recall that sanctity is not a zero-sum game with absolute winners and losers. Holiness, or at least the call to strive for holiness, is a universal calling shared by all women and men. Drawing on the wisdom of the Second Vatican Council's Dogmatic Constitution on the Church, *Lumen Gentium*, the pope is quick to assure us that, "The Holy Spirit bestows holiness in abundance among God's holy and faithful people, for 'it has pleased God to make men and women holy and to save them, not as individuals without any bond between them, but rather as a people who might acknowledge him in truth and serve him in holiness'" (GE 6).[2] This is an important passage for two reasons: holiness is something we are all called to, and we do not achieve holiness alone. Both of these themes are worth unpacking a little.

First, Pope Francis is reinforcing church teaching that explains that holiness is not reserved for a select few. He states this more clearly later in this chapter when addressing each of us and explaining that to be holy "does not require being a bishop, a priest or a religious. We are frequently tempted to think that holiness is

> Holiness is something we are all called to, and we do not achieve holiness alone.

only for those who can withdraw from ordinary affairs to spend much time in prayer." As the pope makes clear, "This is not the case. We are all called to be holy by living our lives with love and by bearing witness in everything we do, wherever we find ourselves" (GE 14). The condition that makes our holiness possible is the universal gift of God's self as Spirit. Our response to God's gift of this grace in every moment of every day and in every place we find ourselves is what it means to live a holy Christian life. Pope Francis provides numerous examples in this section to illustrate this point. He talks about consecrated religious, married couples, laborers, parents, grandparents, and community leaders.

This call to holiness that originates in our baptism is not something that is accomplished merely by performing one or two big and heroic gestures. For most people the path to holiness, to living the way God intends us to live, occurs through small gestures, little decisions, how we shape our attitudes, and what we do for one another. Here we might think of the great wisdom of Mother Teresa of Calcutta, India, who was fond of saying that each of us may not each be able to do grand, large sacrificial gestures, but we can each "do small things with great love."[3] What we do when we are in the checkout line at the grocery store or how we respond to the request from a stranger for assistance or how we surrender our own interest to be present to a loved one who is ill or struggling—these are indeed small things, but small things that invite us to practice showing Christian love.

Holiness does not look the same for everybody. Recalling the multitude of stories that come from the lives of the canonical saints, Pope Francis reminds us: "There are some testimonies that may prove helpful and inspiring, but that we are not meant to copy, for that could even lead us astray from the one specific path that the Lord has in mind for us." He adds, "The important thing is that each believer discern his or her own path, that they bring out the very best of themselves, the most personal gifts that God has placed in their hearts, rather than hopelessly trying to

imitate something not meant for them" (GE 11). On this point,
I recall something attributed to Pope Francis's namesake, St.
Francis of Assisi. It is said that near the end of St. Francis's life,
as he lay dying surrounded by those who loved him, he addressed
his brother friars with an instruction: "The Lord has shown me
what was mine to do, may the Lord show you what is yours."[4]
St. Francis did not believe that God wanted those inspired by his
life and ministry to copy exactly how he lived and what he did in
this life. God does not need us to be another St. Francis—God
needs us to become saints ourselves! As if to flesh out this point,
the pope provides a hypothetical example of a day in the life of
an ordinary woman whose holiness is reflected in responding to
the circumstances of her particular context.

> Here is an example: a woman goes shopping, she meets a neighbor and they begin to speak, and the gossip starts. But she says in her heart: "No, I will not speak badly of anyone." This is a step forward in holiness. Later, at home, one of her children wants to talk to her about his hopes and dreams, and even though she is tired, she sits down and listens with patience and love. That is another sacrifice that brings holiness. Later she experiences some anxiety, but recalling the love of the Virgin Mary, she takes her rosary and prays with faith. Yet another path of holiness. Later still, she goes out onto the street, encounters a poor person and stops to say a kind word to him. One more step. (GE 16)

Holiness does not look the same for everybody.

While there are admittedly some cultural stereotypes underlying
this particular example, the general point about the daily, particular, and small gestures along the path to holiness is well taken.
We can all relate to times when we have had the opportunity to
indulge in gossip or "vent" about someone who has annoyed or

angered us. What do we choose to do in that instance? We can all relate to the experience of being tired and desiring nothing more than to be alone or seek some peace and quiet when another person needed us. How do we respond to that person? We can all relate to the choice before us when we are confronted by the need of a stranger who might ask us for some assistance or, at the very least, recognition that he or she simply exists. Do we take the time to acknowledge the dignity and value of the person in our midst? Each and every day these little choices reflect our willingness—or lack thereof—to respond to God's invitation to Christian holiness.

Second, Pope Francis reminds us that our path to holiness is never an independent or individual process. Just as we receive our primary vocation to Christian holiness at baptism, we also enter into a community, which we call the Body of Christ. "We are never completely ourselves unless we belong to a people," the pope says. "That is why no one is saved alone, as an isolated individual. Rather, God draws us to himself, taking into account the complex fabric of interpersonal relationships present in a human community" (GE 6). This sense of community, which we call the church, is founded on the example that God gives us in Jesus Christ. Furthermore, God did not wish for us to form a community merely among ourselves. Rather, God desired to enter into this very same community through the incarnation, as Pope Francis reiterates: "God wanted to enter into the life and history of a people" (GE 6). So important is community, relationship, connection, family, and love that God planned to be a part of this community from all eternity and became flesh to share in this life.

This central element of Christian life—community—is something that Pope Francis has spent a fair amount of time discussing in earlier writings. In his earlier apostolic exhortation, *Evangelii Gaudium* ("The Joy of the Gospel," hereafter EG), the pope explains that, like the call we have received to pursue holiness, we have also received a call from Christ to be messengers of the Good News to the whole world. "In our day Jesus' command to 'go and make disciples' echoes in the changing scenarios and ever new challenges to the Church's mission of evangelization, and all of us are called to take part in this new missionary 'going forth'. Each Christian and every community must discern the path that the Lord points out, but all of us are asked to obey his call to go forth from our own comfort zone in order to reach all the 'peripheries' in need of the light of the Gospel" (EG 20).

It's not enough to respond to this call individually, but we are called as a community of believers, the Body of Christ. Holiness is found in responding to the needs of those we meet, but it also involves going out into the margins to meet people where they are and therefore requires of us taking the risk to go out beyond the limits of what we find comfortable and safe. This rightly appears as a daunting task, but drawing on the insights of the New Zealand bishops, the pope reminds us that "just to try to love as Christ loved us shows that Christ shares his own risen life with us. In this way, our lives demonstrate his power at work—even in the midst of human weakness" (GE 18).[5]

Far too often many Christians see holiness as an individual trait achieved by this or that extraordinary person. And yet, Jesus always called people into relationship, into community, into dialogue with others. It's one thing to reflect on the ways we are or are not saying yes to God. It is another thing to ask questions of our faith community more broadly and ask if we are doing our own part to facilitate the mission and ministry of Christ in our world. Here we might think of the admonition of St. Paul to the Romans where he reminds the early Christians and us today: "Let us then pursue what leads to peace and to building up one another" (14:19). This value stands in stark contrast with what so many of our cultures and societies encourage us to embrace.

It's not that we are actively discouraged from participating in communal activities and associations, but instead such pursuits are often intended to serve us as individuals. This worldly wisdom encourages us to ask: "What am *I* getting out of being a part of this group?" In contrast, the wisdom of God seen in Scripture and throughout Pope Francis's exhortation encourages us to ask: "How am I working with others to build up the Kingdom of God for the benefit of all people?"

We can think of the last three sections of chapter 1 as Pope Francis's effort to develop the notion of holiness in terms of vocation. Indeed, everyone has received this call in baptism, and this call is something that takes place within and because of the community of the church, but each of us has a unique mission or purpose. In unpacking what it means to talk about Christian holiness, the pope explains that our particular vocations always involve union with Christ, working for the reign of God, and becoming more authentically our true selves. Let's take a closer look at each of these elements.

When thinking about what God is calling us to in life, examining what our ultimate purpose is, we ought to ask ourselves: what is my end goal? Or, what is the right path for me in life? It seems to me, from my personal experience and pastoral ministry, that these sorts of questions are rarely considered in a big overarching way. Typically, women and men ask questions that arise at a given moment and in a particular context. What college should I attend? What field of study should I pursue? What internship is the best for me? Which job offer should I take? Should I marry this person? When is the right time to start a family? And so on. While asking these specific questions is certainly important, the pope is inviting us to consider what *general* compass or orientation point we use to help us discern the correct answer. Pope Francis invites us to think about how each of our particular choices in any given time relates to the ultimate mission to which God has called us. "A Christian cannot think of his or her mission on earth without seeing it as a path of holiness, for 'this is the will of God, your sanctification' (1 Thessalonians 4:3)" (GE 19). In thinking about this broader, ongoing, and lifelong path of holiness to which God has called us, we must always look to Christ as the guide and model.

> That mission has its fullest meaning in Christ, and can only be understood through him. At its core, holiness is experiencing, in union with Christ, the mysteries of his life. It consists in uniting ourselves to the Lord's death and resurrection in a unique and personal way, constantly dying and rising anew with him. But it can also entail reproducing in our own lives various aspects of Jesus's earthly life: his hidden life, his life in community, his closeness to the outcast, his poverty and other ways in which he showed his self-sacrificing love. (GE 20)

We must always look to Christ as the guide and model.

It is here that Pope Francis draws from his formation as a Jesuit and encourages us to consider engaging our imaginations in prayer and discernment. When reflecting on questions about how we ought to live and what we ought to do, can we place ourselves in the narratives of the Gospel? It has become a cliché to ask "what would Jesus do," but there remains some wisdom in asking ourselves what *did* Jesus do in order to ground our own choices and actions. It's not that Pope Francis envisions each of us becoming little replicas of Jesus of Nazareth. Rather, it's a matter of becoming a person whose own compass is oriented to Christ in order that we may each become the person God intends us to be. This is what it means to pursue a life of Christian holiness.

In an age when individualism and indifference to the experiences of others are two major threats, and these are concerns about which the Holy Father speaks often, it can seem counterintuitive to explore greater meaning in our lives apart from what is immediately satisfying or seemingly advantageous for each of us personally. Yet, we are told that true peace and satisfaction is found only when our own life aligns with God's plan for us. "Always ask the Spirit what Jesus expects from you at every moment of your life and in every decision you make, so as to discern its place in the mission you have received" (GE 23). In doing this, we draw nearer to Christ and can become his true disciples in the world. But, as the pope reminds us, this requires a shift in our thinking and our attitudes. "Let yourself be transformed. Let yourself be renewed by the Spirit, so that this can happen, lest you fail in your precious mission. The Lord will bring it to fulfillment despite your mistakes and missteps, provided that you do not abandon the path of love but remain ever open to his supernatural grace, which purifies and enlightens" (GE 24).

In addition to uniting with Christ to discover our true mission or vocation, Pope Francis also explains that every one of us, regardless of our respective social locations and particular callings, is meant to contribute to the in-breaking of God's reign. "Your identification with Christ and his will involves a commitment to build with him that kingdom of love, justice and universal peace" (GE 25). One of the things the pope is challenging in this section is our propensity toward compartmentalizing our lives. Many Christians are content to recall their faith for one hour or so each week when gathered for Mass on Sunday. Perhaps you are someone whose devotional life extends beyond the weekly liturgy to include personal prayer and private meditation. Such activities are good and important. A life that strives toward holiness is, however, one that incorporates everything. "Everything can be accepted and integrated into our life in this world, and become a part of our path to holiness. We are called to be contemplatives even in the midst of action, and to grow in holiness by responsibly and generously carrying out our proper mission" (GE 26).

In a way that anticipates the next chapter, in which the pope addresses what holiness is not and some persistent challenges to living a life of holiness, he mentions briefly in this section that those who feel compelled to "appear holy" or perform certain pious or scrupulous activities in order to impress others, bolster their pride, or alleviate their anxiety about being sufficiently Christian are not practicing authentic holiness (GE 28). This is an important message to those who are inclined to judge themselves or others by outward signs or appearances. One could "look" holy and in fact be very far away from what God desires of us. There are numerous times in the gospels when Jesus also warns his followers of this disconnect. Recall the narrative about the Pharisee and the tax collector at the temple: Which one "looks" holy by outward appearances? Which one actually is holy in action? Recall the parable in Matthew's gospel of the father who instructs his two sons to go work in his field. The first says he will but then does not; the second says he will not but ultimately does. Which one actually is holy in action?

The way around the superficiality of holiness is to develop one's prayer life. Pope Francis tells us that we must seek out "moments of quiet, solitude and silence before God" (GE 29). Echoing the profound wisdom of Thomas Merton, the pope connects our embrace of solitude and discovery of God with our coming to discover our "true selves."[6] Too many distractions and external forces threaten to prevent us from discovering who we are meant to be. The only way we can come to know who we really are is to come to know God, for it is God who has lovingly brought each of us into existence and created us with our particular mission. We are encouraged to form an integrated understanding of our faith and the quest for holiness, one that does not separate out the would-be sacred from the seemingly profane but rather recognizes that "every minute of our lives can be a step along the path to growth in holiness" (GE 31).

Pope Francis closes this chapter with an exhortation to not be afraid of embracing the call to discover our "true selves" or, as he puts it alternatively, "your deepest self" (GE 32). He recounts the harrowing story of St. Josephine Bakhita, the Sudanese-born woman who was kidnapped and sold into slavery when she was seven years old. For decades she was tortured, abused, and dehumanized. When she was eventually freed, she entered religious life as a Canossian sister and shared her story throughout Italy about the hope she found in Jesus Christ amid the unthinkable atrocities and indignities she had faced. St. Josephine provides us with an extreme example of absolute dependence on God. Given the horrendous experience she faced, it would strike many of us as a miracle that she had any faith in God or humanity. And yet, as Pope Francis suggests, the stories of the saints reveal to us that the more dependent we are on God, the closer we draw to the Lord, the more we rely on the Holy Spirit—the more we experience true freedom. So many of the messages we receive from our technologically saturated and consumer-driven world tell us that we must construct our own identities, forge our own paths, do what we want, and assert ourselves at all costs. The message of *Gaudete et Exsultate*, summarizing the message of the Gospel, is quite the opposite. It is only in pursuing a life of holiness that comes from union with Christ, using our gifts in working for the Kingdom of God, and discovering who we are in God that we come to recognize who it is that we were created to be.

Suggestions for Prayer

1. Consider one of the passages from the gospels in which Jesus is addressing his disciples. Imagine yourself in that setting, picture yourself hearing the voice of Jesus speak to you and your circumstances today. What is Jesus asking of you? What are you being encouraged to change or do?

2. Reflect on who has been a "saint next door" in your life—a family member, a friend, a coworker, a stranger—and consider what about their life encourages you to be a better Christian. If the person is living, say a prayer of gratitude for them. If the person is deceased, pray for them and for their intercession.

Reflection Questions

1. How have you thought of holiness throughout your life? Was holiness something you considered reserved for a select few or something toward which all people should strive?

2. What are the ways that you are resistant to God's call to holiness? Do you feel unworthy of such a call? Frightened by such a call?

3. What role does God play in your decision making? How can you better align your life with the narrative of Christ? How can you better incorporate the Holy Spirit in your prayer life?

2 Two Subtle Enemies of Holiness

In the last chapter, we looked at how Pope Francis opens *Gaudete et Exsultate* with an affirmation of the universal call to holiness that all women and men have received in baptism. He goes to great lengths, by description and illustration, to highlight what authentic Christian holiness—or at least the path toward it—looks like. In the second chapter, the pope shifts gears to address challenges to holiness. These challenges are masks that present themselves to some in the world as what holiness looks like, but they are lies and, as Pope Francis explains, repackaged forms of ancient heresies. To some readers this chapter of the apostolic exhortation might appear unnecessarily esoteric. The pope dedicates his focus to gnosticism and pelagianism, which he calls "two false forms of holiness that can lead us astray" (GE 35). If you have never heard of these two heresies, do not worry; you're not alone. Intimidating as the technical theological terms might appear, the concepts they describe are both understandable and relatable once we have broken down their meaning, which we will do in this chapter.

Before exploring these two "false forms of holiness" in their particularity, it may be worth examining the context in which Pope Francis identifies them. At one level, he is addressing what he recognizes as a perennial human struggle for security. Women and men, over the millennia, have sought security and stability in material, emotional, and physical ways. So too, he notes, do people desire what we might call a "spiritual security." For some people, this drive to keep things seemingly simple and unchanging, sure and safe, has led to an unhealthy approach to church doctrine and discipline. Quoting his earlier apostolic exhortation *Evangelii Gaudium*, Pope Francis explains that such efforts to obtain doctrinal or disciplinary security can lead to "a narcissistic and authoritarian elitism, whereby instead of evangelizing, one analyzes and classifies others, and instead of opening the door to grace, one exhausts his or her energies in inspecting and verifying. In neither case is one really concerned about Jesus Christ or others" (EG 94).

What Pope Francis is identifying here is the presence of Christians throughout the world who behave more like a self-appointed doctrinal or liturgical police, who become more concerned with whether or not everybody interprets the faith or worships in their preferred style than with whether or not they are reflecting the love of Christ in their own words and deeds. This sort of behavior has become all the more common thanks to the immediacy and worldwide access to communication that the internet and social media provide us with today. In a keynote address delivered after receiving a prestigious media award in 2016, Father Thomas Rosica, CSB, who founded the Canadian Catholic television network *Salt+Light* and has served in the Vatican's communication office, offered a direct, bold, and accurate assessment of the kinds of people Pope Francis is thinking of here. Fr. Rosica said: "Often times the obsessed, scrupulous, self-appointed, nostalgia-hankering virtual guardians of faith or of liturgical practices are very disturbed, broken and angry individuals, who never found a platform or pulpit in real life and so resort to the Internet and become trolling pontiffs and holy executioners!"[1] As startling as this description may appear, we all know people—in person or online—who fit this description. At various points, we may have been such people ourselves.

On the one hand, Pope Francis is recognizing that women and men who fit these sorts of descriptions are oftentimes people who do genuinely desire to be good Christians. They are after a kind of holiness, but despite their best efforts they are not accurately pursuing Christian holiness. On the other hand, Pope Francis wishes to diagnose some of what causes such behavior that leads to judgment, anger, and vitriol within the church. His proposal of the persistence of gnosticism and pelagianism in our modern age is an effort to get at the root of this trouble and therefore give name to a real temptation many Christians face in seeking to live an authentically holy life.

"Contemporary Gnosticism"

Have you ever heard that what really matters for Christians is not your body but your soul? Have you ever looked with disdain at the physical world or your material body? Have you ever considered that what is important for salvation was only revealed to those closest to Jesus and that information has been passed down to a select group of people over the centuries? If any of these things strike you as sensible or attractive, then you might be an unwitting but good candidate for gnosticism.

The term itself is admittedly vague. Gnosticism is not so much a particular religious or philosophical belief system as a genre of many different traditions over the centuries. The Greek word *gnosis* simply means "knowledge." The particular kind of knowledge gnosticism promotes is understood as that which contributes to the liberation of the spirit or, in Christian terms, the soul from the material body. Though gnosticism is not exclusively tied to Christianity, in the early centuries of the church many gnostic sects emerged around nascent Christian communities. This was one effect of the mingling of cultures in the Mediterranean world at the time of Christianity's origins. Some early Christians who lived in a Greek philosophical and cultural context (oftentimes referred to as "Hellenism") interpreted the teachings of Christianity through a lens that led to gnosticism. In general, gnostics believe in a dualistic world wherein God, who is all good, perfect, loving, etc., created all things spiritual but did not have anything to do directly with the physical, material, and passing world. Divinity and creation were seen as completely oppositional, with the divine and spiritual realm being good and the material realm being evil. Furthermore, because this material world consists of death, suffering, and imperfection, gnostics believed that an all-loving and good God could not possibly be responsible for it. Therefore, gnostics held that there must have been some other, lesser god (a "demiurge") who made this imperfect and material world. This outlook held that our souls, which were created by God, are trapped in this evil material world and must be liberated. The means for such liberation comes through that special knowledge (*gnosis*).

It does not take much imagination to see how Christianity would be attractive to those who espoused this sort of cultural and philosophical disposition. If one were looking for some kind of special knowledge to escape this material world, what better source could you have than a messenger that was understood to be the Son of God? Though these gnostic Christians did not believe that Jesus Christ was as fully divine as God the Creator (that's where the "consubstantial with the Father" of the Creed comes in, as a direct response to the gnostic heresy), they nevertheless accepted that the message of Christ was the highest form of *gnosis*. Furthermore, not only did Christ provide important spiritual teachings to the public about God and right living, but gnostics also believed that he provided "secret knowledge" to his apostles and those in his inner circle of followers that was to be passed down to the elite members of gnostic sects.

From early on Christian theologians and pastoral leaders fought against this way of misunderstanding Christianity. Some of the most significant early Christian theological treatises were focused on the threat that gnosticism presented to authentic Christian belief. Great theologians like St. Irenaeus of Lyons (d. ca. 200) and St. Athanasius of Alexandria (d. 373) wrote whole books in defense of the goodness of creation, the validity of the incarnation, the fact that God created "all things *visible* and *invisible*," and other tenets of authentic Christian faith skewed or rejected by gnostic tendencies. While gnosticism has its origins at the time of the early church, it never really went away. Various gnostic-like misunderstandings of Christianity have appeared on the scene over the centuries—including in our own time. And this is what Pope Francis wishes to address in the first part of chapter 2.

What Pope Francis sees as the threat of "contemporary gnosticism" is twofold. First, there is this tendency of gnosticism to elevate the intellectual or "spiritual" and denigrate the material or physical. Second, gnosticism presents itself as an elite movement wherein only a few are chosen by God to receive the "authentic" knowledge necessary to be liberated or saved. On both fronts, the pope rejects any views or behaviors that promote these errors. The reason Pope Francis sees gnosticism as so problematic today is that many within the Christian community purportedly (if at times unknowingly) embrace this outlook as indicative of holiness. The Holy Father explains: "Gnosticism exercises a deceptive attraction for some people, since the gnostic approach is strict and allegedly pure, and can appear to possess a certain harmony or order that encompasses everything" (GE 38).

To correct the mistaken view that gnostic approaches to understanding Christianity reflect a kind of purity or holiness, the pope calls Christians to return to the basics of our faith and the actual model of Jesus Christ. Here we are reminded that "a person's perfection is measured not by the information or knowledge they possess, but by the depth of their charity" (GE 37). In a manner that rightly indicts practicing Christians and church leaders, teachers, and theologians in particular, *Gaudete et Exsultate* calls out those who think that they understand the faith fully and can articulate the Gospel comprehensibly (GE 38). It is hubris, a kind of religious arrogance, that leads certain Christians into thinking that "they know it all" and that others, especially those whose education or even intellectual aptitude is not as impressive as another's might be, are entirely in the dark or are of lesser sanctity. Here Pope Francis draws on the example of the great Franciscan theologian and doctor of the church St. Bonaventure (d. 1274). Even though this Franciscan saint was a brilliant intellectual and renowned theologian, he always took care to ground his theological work in the authentic humility Jesus models for us in the Gospel and that St. Francis of Assisi embraced throughout his life. Bonaventure believed that true wisdom was reflected in the holiness seen through the way we love one another and embody the Christian message, and this prioritization of love over knowledge as the starting point for theology is seen in his writing and those of many others in the Franciscan intellectual school of the Middle Ages.

In a footnote that is easy to overlook, the pope cites a passage from the end of Bonaventure's spiritual treatise, *Journey of the Soul into God*, in which the doctor of the church talks about how the process of true holiness will require that we surrender our intellectual pursuits in order to direct toward God our deepest and total love. He adds that our natural ability to "understand" the mysteries of God, even for those who are the most intellectually astute, is essentially helpless; therefore, "little importance should be given to [intellectual] investigation and much to unction; little to speech but much to interior joy; little to words or writing and all to the gift of God, namely the Holy Spirit; little or no importance should be given to the creature but all to the creative essence, the Father and the Son and the Holy Spirit."[2] It is an important reminder from the saints, especially those renowned for their intellectual accomplishments such as is seen in the writings of St. Bonaventure or St. Thomas Aquinas, that what fundamentally matters in the life of Christian holiness is how we act and love and not what we think or write.

> What fundamentally matters in the life of Christian holiness is how we act and love and not what we think or write.

This exhortation is especially timely in our digital age when there is a clear lack of charity, kindness, and support online and a whole lot of self-righteousness, selfishness, and intellectual snobbery. Much like the political discourse in our modern American context, the way religion and moral issues are discussed online—and the relative holiness of individuals is addressed—is extremely disheartening. Too often self-identified "good" or "faithful" or "traditional" Catholics adopt a stance of rigidity or absolutism toward the faith that never moves from the head to the heart. Pope Francis warns of this sort of behavior, observing: "When somebody has an answer for every question, it is a sign that they are not on the right road. They may well be false prophets, who use religion for their own purposes, to promote their own psychological or intellectual theories" (GE 41). Without acknowledging the irony, so much hostility and acrimony surfaces over matters that Jesus would decry as irrelevant or at least certainly never justify with such vitriol and hatred.

Those who are inclined toward a contemporary gnosticism that sees right answers and clear truths as justifying judgmental and divisive means of communication presume, the pope says, to know better than God. "Someone who wants everything to be clear and sure presumes to control God's transcendence" (GE

41). Such people are misguided in their self-confidence about how God acts, where God is found, and in whom God is present in the world. They forget, Pope Francis says, that "God is mysteriously present in the life of every person, in a way that he himself chooses, and we cannot exclude this by our presumed certainties" (GE 42). On this point, the pope is speaking to the second threat contemporary gnosticism poses to Christians, namely, the desire for a smaller, elite, and "more pure" church. Such contemporary gnostics are inclined to weaponize the sacraments, claiming to know who is and is not worthy to receive the Eucharist or be present in the assembly. Such contemporary gnostics are poised to kick out of the church those who struggle with their faith or with living a life aligned with the Gospel. But, as Pope Francis said in his 2013 interview with Jesuit Father Antonio Spadaro, "The thing the church needs most today is the ability to heal wounds and to warm the hearts of the faithful; it needs nearness, proximity. I see the church as a field hospital after battle."[3] In that same interview, Pope Francis foreshadowed his exhortation *Gaudete et Exsultate* in elaborating on one of the challenges he sees within the church today:

> The church sometimes has locked itself up in small things, in small-minded rules. The most important thing is the first proclamation: Jesus Christ has saved you. And the ministers of the church must be ministers of mercy above all. The confessor, for example, is always in danger of being either too much of a rigorist or too lax. Neither is merciful, because neither of them really takes responsibility for the person. The rigorist washes his hands so that he leaves it to the commandment. The loose minister washes his hands by simply saying, "This is not a sin" or something like that. In pastoral ministry we must accompany people, and we must heal their wounds.[4]

When we are more concerned about the small-minded rules and who is "right" and who is "wrong" about their interpretation of a particular aspect of the Christian faith and when we forget the bigger picture of the Christian proclamation that "God is love" (1 John 4:8) and has called us to "love one another as I have loved you" (John 13:34), then we have missed the point altogether.

Pope Francis ends this section on gnosticism with a reference to his namesake, St. Francis of Assisi. He quotes a brief letter that St. Francis wrote to St. Anthony of Padua. No, it was not a request for St. Anthony's intercession to help find lost keys. In fact, St. Anthony's primary ministry during his life as a Franciscan friar was to teach theology to the new friars preparing for ministry. Think of him less as someone keen to assist in finding lost items and more like a medieval seminary professor. St. Francis writes in this letter: "I am pleased that you teach sacred theology to the brothers provided that, as is contained in the Rule, you 'do not extinguish the Spirit of prayer and devotion' during study of this kind."[5] The reference St. Francis makes in his letter to what was "contained in the Rule" is an allusion to the Franciscan Rule or way of life. St. Francis instructed all those who desired to be friars to avoid idleness, which is "the enemy of the soul," and that in their work they "do not extinguish the Spirit of holy prayer and devotion to which all temporal things must contribute."[6] One of the things Pope Francis realizes, as St. Francis did before him, is that we can sometimes get "stuck in our heads" and become disconnected from our embodied existence as relational creatures of God. Temptation to become workaholics or addicted to social media and the internet in our digital age are but two common examples of how contemporary gnosticism interrupts our relational lives with one another and with God. This is what it means to extinguish the Spirit of prayer and devotion.

Rather than striving to create a smaller, more elite church shaped in our own image and likeness, Pope Francis is reminding us of the large and welcoming tent of faith Christ has established in his Body, which is the church. Indeed, we may all be at different points in our respective pilgrimages of Gospel living, but we can welcome one another, encourage one another, respectfully challenge and love one another in a way that celebrates not only the intellect but also the heart, not only the perfect but also everybody struggling along the way.

"Contemporary Pelagianism"

The second contemporary challenge to authentic Christian holiness, what Pope Francis calls a "false form of holiness" (GE 35), is known as pelagianism. The pope ties pelagianism to gnosticism at the outset of this section of the chapter, stating, "As time passed, many came to realize that it is not knowledge that betters us or makes us saints, but the kind of life we lead" (GE 47). In a sense pelagianism and gnosticism are related, insofar as both emerged from within the context of the early Christian communities shaped as they were by Hellenistic thought and culture and that both heresies are distortions of Christianity that get *part of the tradition* correct but mistake that part for the whole of Christian teaching. Whereas gnosticism takes the truth that we are more than material beings and distorts that reality into a dualistic worldview that says all that is good and truly matters is the spiritual or intellectual, pelagianism takes the truth that we are responsible for our actions in exercising our free will and distorts that fact into a position that essentially claims we can achieve sanctity or justification before God all on our own.

While gnosticism has an ambiguous origin and has served as a stand-in term for a variety of heretical views over the course of Christian history, pelagianism gets its name from an ancient British monk named Pelagius (d. ca. 520 CE). A contemporary of St. Augustine of Hippo, Pelagius was a Christian who, in many ways, attempted to defend Christianity from gnostic attacks. You may recall that gnostics believe that only a select few, those who have the special knowledge or *gnosis*, were the "real Christians" and therefore could be saved. Pelagius believed that all the baptized had the capacity to be saved. He believed that every person had the capacity necessary to be saved, provided they exercised self-discipline and directed their free will for the good. So far, this doesn't sound so bad, does it? In truth, Pelagius was trying to be inclusive, which is certainly a good thing and up to this point his teaching is generally orthodox.

Where Pelagius went astray was in his misunderstanding of the meaning of divine grace. St. Augustine and the early theologians in the Eastern Churches understood grace to be the divine gift of God's very self as Holy Spirit. Think of the image of Pentecost when God gives the gift of the Holy Spirit to the first disciples. We can talk about various effects of divine grace, but grace is primarily the Holy Spirit. Pelagius identified grace not with the Holy Spirit but with free will, arguing that the gift God gives to humanity is the freedom to choose good or evil for ourselves. To put the difference simply, St. Augustine taught that even our ability to choose the good was itself a gift and a possibility made real only by God's grace. To see how this manifests itself in the prayers of our eucharistic liturgy, consider the "Common Preface IV," which includes the line: "For, although you have no need of our praise, yet our thanksgiving [praise] is itself your gift."[7] One of the effects of God's self-gift to us as Holy Spirit is our ability to choose the good, to do the right, and to offer fitting praise to God. Without God's grace, we couldn't do that.

In effect, Pelagius rejects that teaching. He believed that we could choose the good, do the right, and offer fitting praise to God without God's assistance—we could do all of this on our own. Some time later, a kind of pelagianism emerged that was something of a compromise between St. Augustine's claim of total dependence on God and pelagianism's assertion that we were completely capable on our own. This view became known as "semi-pelagianism," which Pope Francis references in passing without explanation in his apostolic exhortation. Semi-pelagianism accepted most of what St. Augustine taught but still wanted to maintain that human beings have to offer some kind of response to God independent of grace. Two church synods and the Council of Trent would eventually condemn Pelagius's view, the teachings of "pelagianism" that arose as the result from the followers of Pelagius (like Celestius and Julian of Eclanum) taking Pelagius's views to their logical and extreme conclusions, and the semi-pelagianism that followed. The church's basic assertion is that the effects of original sin stay with us even after its presence is cleared at baptism. And because of these effects, we cannot exercise our free will without the gift of God's grace working in and through us from the outset. The key here is an affirmation of our radical dependence on God for salvation. Or, as Pope Francis summarizes this: "It was forgotten that everything 'depends not on human will or exertion, but on God who shows mercy' (Rom 9:16) and that 'he first loved us' (cf. 1 Jn 4:19)" (GE 48). With that basic history and understanding of what is meant by pelagianism, we can turn to *Gaudete et Exsultate* to see how this ancient heresy manifests itself in our contemporary era.

This section draws heavily from the pope's earlier apostolic exhortation *Evangelii Gaudium*, in which we are reminded that those who adopt this sort of pelagian or semi-pelagian worldview "ultimately trust only in their own powers and feel superior to others because they observe certain rules or remain intransigently faithful to a particular Catholic style" (EG 94). Here the pope is addressing those self-identified Catholics who accuse others of being, for example, so-called cafeteria Catholics or not reflecting in thought or practice what they envision Catholicism ought to look like. Such attitudes are not signs of holiness but reflections of arrogance about the perfection of one's own faith and a condescension that belittles the faith journey of others. Again citing St. Bonaventure, the Holy Father notes that each person is at a different point in their Christian pilgrimage and that everybody faces their own challenges and struggles with their respective gifts and strengths. He refers to a paragraph in the Catechism that reminds the faithful that circumstances, context, and history must be taken into consideration when examining the life of another. The single-line paragraph reads: "Imputability and responsibility for an action can be diminished or even nullified by ignorance, inadvertence, duress, fear, habit, inordinate attachments, and other psychological or social factors" (no. 1735).[8] Those who espouse a kind of "contemporary pelagianism" are inclined to believe that their righteousness (or, better, *self-righteousness*) is thanks to themselves alone and that those who may struggle or fall along the way of faith are, therefore, always and entirely responsible for what is perceived as failure or disappointment too.

What is called for here in the quest for true holiness is the humility to accept that anything we do that is good or right can be attributed to God's grace, for without it we can do nothing (GE 51). Coming to terms with the fact that we depend on the generosity of God's grace in accomplishing the good, that we don't do it all ourselves, should help us to be patient and supportive of our sisters and brothers wherever they find themselves. "Ultimately, the lack of a heartfelt and prayerful acknowledgement of our limitations prevents grace from working more effectively within us, for no room is left for bringing about the potential good that is part of a sincere and genuine journey of growth" (GE 50).

Pope Francis reiterates the church's longstanding teaching that we are not justified by our actions, works, or efforts, but by the grace of God (GE 52). At the time of the sixteenth-century Reformations, when the Roman Catholic Church and Martin Luther debated how we are justified alongside concerns about corruption in church practice, there was a misperception on both sides that led to a commonly held belief that Catholics do in fact believe in a kind of "works righteousness." It was understood by the average "Catholic in the pew" that as long as you participated regularly in the sacraments and lived an upstanding life, you'd more or less "earn" a place in heaven. Sadly, this is a superficial and distorted view of the church's teaching. Centuries after the great Reformations, the Roman Catholic Church and the Lutheran World Federation promulgated the Joint Declaration on the Doctrine of Justification in which a mutual understanding was reached that it was by God's free gift of grace that we are justified.[9] Pope Francis summarizes this point by inviting us to recall that God's "friendship infinitely transcends us; we cannot buy it with our works, it can only be a gift born of his loving initiative" (GE 54).

This does not mean that our actions or choices do not matter. That is certainly not the case. Rather, it is recognition that our sanctity, our holiness, is not exclusively our doing or the result of our own will. God is the one who acts first in reaching out to us, inviting us into relationship, empowering us with the gift of the Holy Spirit, which enables us to choose the good, do the right, and give praise in return to God in prayer.

The pope applies this temptation to embrace a kind of pelagianism to our contemporary context by highlighting the insidious ways it appears in the lives of otherwise well-meaning Christians. He says that those who fancy themselves better than or more holy than others because of their "good works" or "commitment to a kind of Catholic culture" find that the "result is a self-centered and elitist complacency, bereft of true love" (GE 57). He warns that too often instead of allowing the Holy Spirit to guide them in the path of love, many of these self-styled Christians begin to bear "an obsession with the law, an absorption with social and political advantages, a punctilious concern for the Church's liturgy, doctrine and prestige, a vanity about the ability to manage practical matters, and an excessive concern with programs of self-help and personal fulfillment" (GE 57). Holiness in this case begins to be mistaken for scrupulousness about rules and laws or, worse still, a political or social game in which one is merely concerned about *appearing holy* rather than *becoming holy*.

I am reminded in this section of *Gaudete et Exsultate* of Pope Francis's namesake, who himself recognized this kind of challenge for his brother friars. St. Francis once spoke to his brothers and addressed the temptation to self-righteousness and pride. His words bring together both contemporary threats of gnosticism and pelagianism with their dual concern with knowledge and will.

> In what, then, can you boast? Even if you were so skillful and wise that you possessed all knowledge, knew how to interpret every kind of language, and to scrutinize heavenly matters with skill: you could not boast in these things. For, even though someone may have received from the Lord a special knowledge of the highest wisdom, one demon knew about heavenly matters and now knows more about those of earth than all human beings. In the same way, even if you were more handsome and richer than everyone else, and even if you worked miracles so that you put demons to flight: all these things are contrary to you; nothing belongs to you; you can boast in none of these things. But we can boast in our weaknesses and in carrying each day the holy cross of our Lord Jesus Christ.[10]

St. Francis's point was to encourage an authentic humility that recognizes the ways that God's grace works in and through us to help bring about the Kingdom of God. The only thing we can rightly take credit for, if we want to put it that way, is our own sinfulness.

Pope Francis shares with us the remedy for these "new forms of gnosticism and pelagianism" that weigh down the church in its path toward holiness. He says that we should first take an honest look at our own lives, in our own hearts, and bring to prayer a true examination of conscience in order to discern whether these false types of holiness may be present in our lives (GE 62). Then the only thing left for us to do is avoid complicating the Gospel and listen to the simple command of Christ to love God and one another, which is possible only with the help of God's grace.

Suggestions for Prayer

> Avoid complicating the Gospel and listen to the simple command of Christ to love God and one another.

1. What do you ask for when you approach God in prayer? In light of this chapter in *Gaudete et Exsultate*, perhaps consider bringing before God a request for greater clarity of discernment in looking over your life, your decisions, and your actions.

2. Reflect on the ways that contemporary gnosticism and pelagianism threaten your own journey of faith and path to holiness. Where are the places you need to grow?

Reflection Questions

1. Where do you see contemporary gnosticism appearing globally, in your society, local community, church, and personal life?

2. Where do you see contemporary pelagianism appearing globally, in your society, local community, church, and personal life?

3. How do you see the digital age with ready access to the internet and social media affecting the presence of what Pope Francis identifies as "false forms of holiness" in our time?

Striving Toward Holiness in the Modern World

Whereas the first part of *Gaudete et Exsultate* focuses on the definition and our understanding of holiness, the second part of the apostolic exhortation is primarily geared toward responding to the unnamed question: "What does Christian holiness look like in practice?" And what better way is there to begin exploring what it means to be holy than to look at what Jesus taught us? Pope Francis opens this section with a lengthy chapter on the teachings of Jesus in general and the Beatitudes in particular (Matt 5:3-12 and Luke 6:20-23). Grounded in the pope's conviction that the Gospel presents to us the essential pattern of what is needed to be good Christians, provided, of course, we don't water down the simple message of Christ, chapter 3 traces the eight hallmarks of what it means to live as a disciple in the world and concludes with the simple yet challenging truth that "Christianity is meant above all to be put into practice" (GE 109).

In many ways, chapter 3 is a reexamination of the tradition, a looking back to the central resources of our faith in the teaching of Jesus Christ. Chapter 4 is a complementary chapter in that Pope Francis shifts gears to look at the present circumstances of being a disciple in the modern world. Here he provides five points for reflection that mark characteristics that the pope sees as necessary to live a way of life in keeping with Christian holiness. These themes are: perseverance, patience, and meekness; joy and a sense of humor; boldness and passion; community; and prayer.

Finally, the pope concludes his apostolic exhortation with a chapter dedicated to what he calls "Spiritual Combat, Vigilance, and Discernment." Admittedly, the first theme might strike contemporary readers as odd or out of tune with the rest of the document. Pope Francis explains, however, that one of the contemporary challenges to Christian holiness in our scientifically advanced and technological age is a kind of rationalism that writes off the reality of evil in the world. In order to pursue a Christian life of holiness, we must be ready for the temptations and stumbling blocks the devil is prepared to place before us. Furthermore, we need to cultivate the virtues of vigilance and discernment if we hope to progress along the path of holiness.

3 In the Light of the Master

Having spent the last two chapters exploring what authentic Christian holiness is and is not, Pope Francis opens this chapter with a basic presupposition that to know what we ought to do and how we ought to live the Christian life, we should turn "to Jesus's words and [see] his way of teaching the truth" (GE 63). This is our source of holiness. Jesus lays the path for us clearly in the Gospel. It is no accident that the early followers of Jesus referred to their emerging religious tradition as "the Way" rather than "Christianity" as we now call our faith.[1] Jesus is not simply to be admired from a distance, appreciated for his exemplary life without any challenge or invitation to conversion in our lives. Instead, while Christ came to reveal to us who God is most fully, he also reveals to us the pattern of life God intends us to live. To understand holiness apart from the path of Jesus Christ—the *Way*—is to mistake something else for Christianity.

Pope Francis suggests that although we should look at Jesus's whole life and ministry, it is the Beatitudes in Matthew (5:3-12) and Luke (6:20-23) that serve as something "like a Christian's identity card" (GE 63). If we want to know what it looks like to be a Christian, then we should look to the activity and attitudes that flow from Jesus's teachings in the Beatitudes. This emphasis on Jesus the teacher is where the chapter title comes from—"In the Light of the Master." Jesus is the true teacher, the "master" (from the Latin *magister*, which means "teacher"), and to be a Christian means to be a lifelong student of this divine teacher. "In the Beatitudes, we find a portrait of the Master, which we are called to reflect in our daily lives" (GE 63).

Before turning to each of the eight Beatitudes, the pope challenges us by saying that we often have a tendency to domesticate or water down the Gospel. Too many of us find Christianity to be something easily compatible with our contemporary cultural contexts or personal priorities and therefore comfortable to live. If we find this to be the case, we may be missing something in the Scripture: either we are misunderstanding the teachings of Jesus or we willfully reinterpret or ignore them so as to avoid inconveniencing ourselves. Stating that the Beatitudes "clearly run counter to the way things are usually done in our world," Pope Francis reminds us that the "Beatitudes are in no way trite or undemanding, quite the opposite." The Gospel is meant to be unsettling, because the message challenges each of us to be better followers of Christ. Because the Christian life is difficult to live when taken seriously, God sends us the gift of grace—the Holy Spirit—with which God "fills us with his power and frees us from our weakness, our selfishness, our complacency and our pride" (GE 65). Pope Francis encourages us to pray for the assistance of the Spirit and invites us to listen to Jesus in order to "allow his words to unsettle us, to challenge us and to demand a real change in the way we live" (GE 66).

> The Gospel is meant to be unsettling, because the message challenges each of us to be better followers of Christ.

1. "Blessed Are the Poor in Spirit"

Some years ago I lived in a large community of Franciscan friars that ministered in the heart of downtown Boston. The church—St. Anthony Shrine and Ministry Center—was a hub of sacramental, pastoral, and charitable service, and those of us who lived and worked there ministered to people from all walks of life. At one point while I was in residence there, construction began on a sixty-floor skyscraper that would sit just a block from our church and ministry site. It was slated to be predominantly residential, which was exciting for a part of the city that was really occupied only by businesspeople and tourists during the workday and was largely silent at night and on weekends. I recall over dinner the excitement the friars expressed—myself included—at the prospect of so many new residents moving in to this part of the city and so close to the church. Surely, we mused, a certain number of the new residents would be Catholic and would bolster our already robust sacramental life. Other friars talked about how this was going to be a boon for our weekly collection. That many of the new residents of this tower would have disposable income was not a question. The top-floor penthouse apartment sold for $37.5 million![2] But then, with both wisdom and a touch of sarcasm, an insightful senior friar spoke up and said: "We'll never see most of those people." The protests erupted over coffee, to which he simply responded: "If you have that much money, you don't *need* God."

Obviously, this friar did not mean anything existential, as if to suggest that some people can go it on their own and are totally independent of God's sustaining of life and existence. Rather, he was getting at the mentality of the wealthy and comfortable (in this case, the *super* wealthy and *extraordinarily* comfortable). Had Pope Francis been at our dining room table, I have no doubt that he would have nodded his head in agreement with my brother Franciscan. In *Gaudete et Exsultate* he says essentially the same thing. "Indeed, once we think we are rich, we can become so self-satisfied that we leave no room for God's word, for the love of our brothers and sisters, or for the enjoyment of the most important things in life" (GE 68). It's not that the wealthy residents of that Boston skyscraper did not actually need God;

it's that they might *think* that they do not need God—or give no thought to God at all.

In looking at Jesus's first Beatitude calling the "poor in spirit" blessed (Matt 5:3), Pope Francis is drawing our attention to the practical demands of the Gospel life. Though most of us could never even imagine spending tens of millions of dollars on an apartment, relative to the rest of the global population we remain exceedingly wealthy. There rests with us a temptation, especially those who occupy social locations of privilege or comfort, to think that we also don't need God or one another. Such an outlook leads to a dulling of our hearts and consciences such that we think more and more about ourselves, securing our wealth, guaranteeing our comfort, and looking toward future personal gains so that we "miss out on the greatest treasure of all" (GE 68). We miss out on the love and relationships that arise from a mutual appreciation of our interdependence on one another and ultimate dependence on God.

One of the ways the pope encourages us to develop this restored sense of Christian interdependence is by cultivating what St. Ignatius Loyola called "holy indifference." This is different from what we typically mean by "indifference" as a kind of laissez-faire disinterest or ambivalence. Holy indifference is similar to what St. Francis of Assisi called *sine proprio* in Latin: to make nothing one's own, to let go, to not possess or hold on to. In both cases, it's a matter of going about the world recognizing that we are not the lords and ladies of creation or other people, as if they were here merely for our use or abuse. We have to use things—food, clothing, shelter, transportation, etc.—but we do not have to dominate these things or seek to possess them for ourselves alone. This is a mentality we must develop and an attitude we have to exercise with practice. Too often the world around us tells us that we are what we have or control. This is not the Gospel message and it is not the way to holiness.

But to be blessed as one who is poor is not simply about a mind-set or an attitude; it also has concrete material implications. Pope Francis points out that Luke's account of the Beatitudes does not add "in spirit" to Jesus's blessing of the poor. Instead, Luke boldly states: "Blessed are the poor" (6:20). This challenges us Christians "to live a plain and austere life" (GE 70). It invites an examination of conscience that seeks to uncover the ways we accumulate things or money that goes above and beyond what is necessary for basic human flourishing. Drawing on the early wisdom figures in the Christian tradition, Dorothy Day would often say: "The bread you retain belongs to the hungry, the garment you lock up is the property of the naked. . . . What is superfluous for one's need is to be regarded as plunder if one retains it for one's self."[3] In other words, to have more than we need is akin to stealing from those who already suffer from not having what they need.

> We have to use things—food, clothing, shelter, transportation, etc.—but we do not have to dominate these things or seek to possess them for ourselves alone.

2. "Blessed Are the Meek"

Pope Francis is not shy about naming our contemporary cultures as contributing to the divisions, hostility, and hatred we witness and experience today. In discussing the need to respond to Jesus's command to be meek, the pope notes that this may seem like an absurd instruction in an age when our cultures encourage selfishness and striving toward what the world perceives as greatness. "Ultimately, it is the reign of pride and vanity, where each person thinks he or she has the right to dominate others." Jesus's message is one that "proposes a different way of doing things: the way of meekness" (GE 71).

So, what is meekness exactly? The way that the pope describes it in this section of the chapter is in terms of negation, what it *is not*. Meekness is not a sense of superiority. Meekness is not an attitude that leads to "conflict, disputes, and enmity on all sides" (GE 71). Meekness is not putting down others because they dress, think, act, or pray differently than you. Meekness is not arrogance or self-centeredness. Meekness is not impatience. Meekness is pacific, that is, peacefulness, but it is not *passive*. Meekness is not about "rolling over" at every occasion and allowing others to take advantage of you. Meekness is certainly not about a stance of weakness.

Meekness
is pacific, that
is, peacefulness,
but it is not
passive.

Those who are meek are people of conviction, faithful women and men who know who God is and who God is calling them to be. But the way they go about living in the world and relating to others is not according to what is too often perceived as strength—bluster, braggadocio, condescension, and the like. The way Jesus calls us to live is modeled in the way he related to others during his earthly ministry. He welcomed everybody, treating the poorest and most marginal people of his time with equal dignity to the highest-class people of his age. Even his parables reflected this call to meekness, as is seen in the story of the wedding invitation in which one is reminded to take the lowest social position rather than assume the highest (Luke 14:7-14).

Pope Francis ties the call to meekness to the embrace of Gospel poverty. "Meekness is yet another expression of the interior poverty of those who put their trust in God alone. Indeed, in the Bible the same word—*anawim*—usually refers both to the poor and to the meek" (GE 74). What is required of us on our path toward holiness is a reconsideration of our attitudes and manner of expressing ourselves. This is all the more true in this digital age when hostility and vitriol shapes nearly every section of the internet and the social media world. How do we express our thoughts and views? How do we respond to people of different backgrounds or with different perspectives? What is Christ calling me to do in living a more holy life? Answering these questions and others like them with a renewed commitment to Christian holiness begins by looking to Jesus for inspiration and guidance. "In every situation," the pope says, "the meek put their hope in the Lord, and those who hope for him shall possess the land . . . and enjoy the fullness of peace (cf. Psalm 37)" (GE 74).

3. *"Blessed Are Those Who Mourn"*

In one striking sentence, Pope Francis summarizes a general sensibility of our time: "The world has no desire to mourn; it would rather disregard painful situations, cover them up or hide them" (GE 75). Certainly, those who are comfortable and secure in an unjust society are often both financially and psychologically able to ignore the plight of those who suffer, those who cry out with lament at injustice. "Much energy is expended on fleeing from situations of suffering in the belief that reality can be concealed" (GE 75). Meanwhile, those women, men, and children who are victims of any kind in our time are afforded no such luxury of escaping the saddening and devastating truths of suffering.

The path to Christian holiness is one that brings us square in the face of suffering. I am reminded of a story that a former Maryknoll lay missioner once told me about his and his wife's return to the United States after some years of service overseas. He recounted the experience of joining his extended family for Thanksgiving at the house of one of his sisters. After an otherwise enjoyable dinner, the family socialized in the living room: adult siblings around couches, their children in the next room playing with toys on the floor. The discussion included hesitant questions about what life had been like in Tanzania, where my friend and his wife had worked. They shared with their family some stories of great joy and happiness but did not shy away from hard truths they witnessed about the suffering of the global poor. It just so happened that my friend had a videocassette with footage of the village where they lived for several years, so he popped it into the VCR, and the land they had called home appeared on the screen before the family. Included in the video were scenes of children who suffered malnutrition and serious illnesses, including childhood HIV/AIDS, and a life that looked not just foreign but nightmarish to some of the first-time viewers. At one point, his sister quickly got up from the couch, went to the television, and promptly turned off the screen. Turning to him, she shouted: "Enough! Don't bring this into my house; I don't want to know about this! I just don't want to know!"

Accustomed to living in the comfort of willful ignorance, this former missioner's sister could not bring herself to accept the reality of those who suffered, even those on the other side of the globe. What she witnessed, confronted as she was by the truth of her brother and sister-in-law's experiences and stories, challenged her to mourn and change her life. She wasn't yet ready, or perhaps willing, to do that.

Pope Francis describes a person on the path to Christian holiness as, in part, being someone open to accepting the reality that others suffer and allowing their suffering to touch one's heart and soul. He explains:

> Such persons are unafraid to share in the suffering of others; they do not flee from painful situations. They discover the meaning of life by coming to the aid of those who suffer, understanding their anguish and bringing relief. They sense that the other is flesh of our flesh, and are not afraid to draw near, even to touch their wounds. They feel compassion for others in such a way that all distance vanishes. In

this way they can embrace St. Paul's exhortation: "Weep with those who weep" (Romans 12:15). (GE 76)

Christian discipleship calls us to be empathetic and seek out those who suffer in order to recognize their pain, fight against injustice, and mourn with them in their mourning. To do anything else is to succumb to what the Bible frequently describes as a "hardened heart."

4. "Blessed Are Those Who Hunger and Thirst for Righteousness"

This particular Beatitude has been one that doesn't get as much attention as some of the others. Pope Francis draws our attention to the intensity of the description, suggesting that we might easily miss the qualifiers "hunger" and "thirst." This Beatitude is Jesus's teaching about the connection between holiness and righteousness, our living a good Christian life and the work of justice and peace in our world. The pope writes, "Hunger and thirst are intense experiences, since they involve basic needs and our instinct for survival" (GE 77). This raises the question: do we long for justice and peace with the yearning and intensity of someone who hasn't eaten all day or is tremendously thirsty?

In addition to the passion for righteousness we are called to live, Pope Francis notes that Jesus also promises satisfaction, that those who long for righteousness with a burning intensity should rest assured that justice and peace will come, even if we do not necessarily see the results in our own lifetime (GE 77). Here we might think of someone like Martin Luther King

> Do we long for justice and peace with the yearning and intensity of someone who hasn't eaten all day or is tremendously thirsty?

Jr., who was tragically assassinated in his thirties for embracing the Christian Beatitudes, working as he did with an intense passion for righteousness. He often reflected in his sermons, speeches, and interviews on the fact that one who "hungers and thirsts for righteousness" may not see the success of those efforts. And yet, we do not quit because we cannot have instant gratification or get the results we would like to see immediately.

Pope Francis explains that the righteousness we hunger and thirst for as Christians pursuing holiness is a kind of peace and justice the world cannot give. "Jesus offers a justice other than that of the world, so often marred by petty interests and manipulated in various ways." "Justice" as understood by the world is often coded language for what the pope calls "the daily politics of *quid pro quo*" (GE 78). Christian holiness rejects this approach and instead follows the teachings of Jesus, who showed that death does not have the last word and that God's vision of success does not align with that of so many people in the world. How do we measure our own success? At what cost do we pursue what our culture, career, family, or friends suggest is success? Pope Francis explains that true success is borne out by the daily choices we make to be faithful to our baptismal calling to walk in the footsteps of Christ in working for justice on behalf of those who are most vulnerable (GE 79).

5. *"Blessed Are the Merciful"*

This Beatitude is certainly a favorite of Pope Francis. Mercy has been a hallmark of the pope's ministry, his preaching, and his actions. So central is the theme of mercy to his understanding of what it means to be a Christian in general and the Bishop of Rome in particular, he dedicated his first official homily as pope to the theme during the liturgy at which he assumed his ministry in a formal way. The opening lines of that homily were: "What a beautiful truth of faith this is for our lives: the mercy of God! God's love for us is so great, so deep; it is an unfailing love, one that always takes us by the hand and supports us, lifts us up, and leads us on."[4] Pope Francis reminds us that all we need to do in order to learn about the kind of mercy God expects from us is to look to God's own example in Jesus Christ. He develops this further in his 2015 document announcing the church's Year of Mercy, *Misericordiae Vultus*: "In short, the mercy of God is not an abstract idea, but a concrete reality through which he reveals his love as that of a father or a mother, moved to the very depths out of love for their child."[5]

The mercy that Jesus calls all Christians to show in the world is not an idea that is removed and remote but embodied and practical. He explains in *Gaudete et Exsultate*: "Mercy has two aspects. It involves giving, helping, and serving others, but it also includes forgiving and understanding" (GE 80). The mercy we show in giving, helping, and serving overlaps with several of the other Beatitudes, which is why the pope focuses most of his attention on forgiveness. This is something he outlined earlier in the document *Misericordiae Vultus*, in which he reminded us that "we are called to show mercy because mercy has been shown to us." Each day God extends to us tremendous mercy, showering us with forgiveness for the big and little transgressions we commit against one another, ourselves, and God. And yet, despite being forgiven time and again by God, we are often so slow to forgive others. Here we might think of Jesus's parable of the wicked servant who, though he was forgiven by his master for a large debt he owed, nevertheless could not forgive another servant for some lesser debt owed to him (Matt 18:23-35). Pope Francis explains: "Pardoning offenses becomes the clearest expression of merciful love, and for us Christians it is

The mercy that Jesus calls all Christians to show in the world is not an idea that is removed and remote but embodied and practical.

an imperative from which we cannot excuse ourselves. At times how hard it seems to forgive!"[6]

Indeed, how difficult forgiveness is!

In his usual lighthearted and poetic way, the pope reminds us that "Jesus does not say, 'Blessed are those who plot revenge'" (GE 82). It is one thing not to forgive others like the wicked servant in the parable, but our popular cultures and worldly values tend to encourage us to "plot revenge" against those who have offended us. Forgiveness in the sense of Christian holiness is not dependent on the response of the one forgiven. And this can be difficult for us to accept. The reason that withholding mercy is a barrier to holiness is not what it does to the other but what it does to us. It is like a weight tied around our necks, a burden that inhibits our free movement as messengers of the Good News. It leads us to be sullen and removed, disinterested and unsympathetic. It gets in the way of living the life of love God calls us to live.

6. *"Blessed Are the Pure in Heart"*

This Beatitude is another one oftentimes misunderstood or overlooked. Pope Francis encourages us to return to Sacred Scripture to uncover insight about what Jesus meant for us. "The Bible uses the heart to describe our real intentions, the things we truly seek and desire, apart from all appearances" (GE 83). This teaching of Jesus is focused on our call to be sincere and forthright about our motives and intentions. Recounting the many times in Scripture that Jesus calls out the hypocrisy of religious leaders who love to *appear* holy, Pope Francis warns us again that the external postures we assume do not fool God. "The Father, 'who sees in secret' (Matthew 6:6), recognizes what is impure and insincere, mere display or appearance, as does the Son" (GE 84).

One way to incorporate this Beatitude into our daily lives as Christians on the path to holiness is to recognize the importance of a regular examination of conscience. Motives are certainly always mixed, but left unchecked we may not be honest with ourselves about the reasons we do this or that thing or make this or that decision. An examination of conscience keeps us honest and allows us to recognize the forgiveness God offers to us. In turn, we can be confident that our efforts to be pure in heart are genuine, and in that sense we continue along the path of discipleship the Lord sets before us.

> The external postures we assume do not fool God.

7. "Blessed Are the Peacemakers"

Christian holiness is marked in part by how willing we are to be truly human. What I mean by this is what St. Francis of Assisi describes in his famous *Canticle of the Creatures* in which he lists various aspects of God's creation, noting the many ways various things in this universe give praise to God. The Sun gives praise to God by shining its rays and providing light; the Earth gives praise to God by providing us with shelter and growing all kinds of vegetation that sustains life. But how do humans give praise to God? St. Francis says: "Praise be You, my Lord, through those who give pardon for Your love, and bear infirmity and tribulation. Blessed are those who endure in peace for by You, Most High, shall they be crowned."[7] What it means to be fully human is to "endure in peace," just as what it means to be fully the Sun is to shine with its rays and give us light. In essence, this teaching of Jesus is one that calls us to be mindful of the core of our being and to recall that God intends us not to be sparring for power or fighting one another but to be peacemakers.

> God intends us not to be sparring for power or fighting one another but to be peacemakers.

Pope Francis acknowledges that most people hear "blessed are the peacemakers" and think immediately of war and violent force. Such people might gloss over this particular Beatitude and think, "Well, I don't fight others, I'm not a physically violent person, I don't use weapons or engage in war--this doesn't apply to me!" Yet, the Holy Father makes an important point: not all war is fought on a battlefield and not all violence is physical. There are many different kinds of violence and activities that plant not peace but "conflict" or "misunderstanding" (GE 87). He provides an example that all of us can relate to, whether in the confines of our family home, our workplace lunchroom, or our religious community. "For example, I may hear something about someone and I go off and repeat it. I may even embellish it the second time around and keep spreading it. . . . And the more harm it does, the more satisfaction I seem to derive from it. The world of gossip, inhabited by negative and destructive people, does not bring peace. Such people are really the enemies of peace" (GE 87).

In pointing to the seemingly mundane, common experience of gossip, Pope Francis is highlighting the challenge of the Gospel in everyday life. He reminds us that violence, war, unrest, and anger begin in the heart and affect the community even if we never take up arms. Living the life of a Christian peacemaker means excluding no one and embracing "even those who are a bit odd, troublesome, or difficult, demanding, different, beaten down by life or simply uninterested. It is hard work" (GE 89). Being Christian peacemakers is something all of us can and must work on—it's a lifelong project.

8. *"Blessed Are Those Who Are Persecuted for Righteousness's Sake"*

Earlier in this chapter Pope Francis reminded us of our call to be so passionate about the work of peace and justice—the quest for righteousness—that it ought to feel as extreme as true hunger or thirst. Examining this last Beatitude, the pope reiterates Jesus's teaching about the cost of true Christian holiness. "Jesus himself warns us that the path he proposes goes against the flow, even making us challenge society by the way we live and, as a result, becoming a nuisance" (GE 90). This risky business of becoming a potential "nuisance" in society and the church is what results from taking seriously the truth that the world's priorities do not align comfortably with those of God. Pope Francis notes that "the Beatitudes are not easy to live out; any attempt to do so will be viewed negatively, regarded with suspicion, and met with ridicule" (GE 91). At best, we risk the vulnerability that paints us as fools; at worst, we risk being persecuted for the sake of the Gospel.

Among those modern prophets who knew what it is like to live this difficult teaching stands Saint Óscar Romero, the martyred archbishop of San Salvador. Like all great prophets, those who preach the word of God and fight against injustice, he did not come to a full sense of his Christian vocation at once. It took time and he learned that Jesus Christ was calling him into greater and greater solidarity with the sheep of his flock who were being abused and persecuted by an unjust government. Reading his writings and homilies is inspiring and challenging. They provide us with a witness to what it looks like to put these teachings of Jesus in action. He said in December 1977: "To be a Christian now means to have the courage to preach the true teaching of Christ and not be afraid of it, not be silent out of fear and preach something easy that won't cause problems."[8] This is often the temptation of well-meaning Christians. We convince ourselves that being a good person, a holy person, means that we don't "ruffle any feathers" or "rock the boat." We are told to be nice guys and gals, to not interfere in the business of others. But such an attitude and behavior results not in increased sanctity;

it results in the production of guilty bystanders who are not any more Christian but are just more complicit.

Fear is at the foundation of many people's hesitancy about embracing the Beatitudes: fear of failure, fear of ridicule, fear of harm or the loss of one's life. But Pope Francis and Archbishop Romero echo the words of Jesus in proclaiming boldly to us: "Do not be afraid!" Near the end of his life, Archbishop Romero began to see with clearer and clearer sight what Christ was calling him and the whole church to do. "Because it is God's work," he once said, "we don't fear the prophetic mission the Lord has entrusted to us. I can imagine someone saying, 'So now he thinks he's a prophet!' No it's not that I think I'm a prophet; it's that you and I are a prophetic people. Everyone baptized has received a share in Christ's prophetic mission."[9]

> Fear is at the foundation of many people's hesitancy about embracing the Beatitudes.

Pope Francis is very honest about the cost of Christian holiness and the risk of persecution that follows. While most Christians today do not face threats of physical violence, there are still some parts of the world in which those who practice their faith openly or work for justice in the name of the Gospel are harmed or killed. For the great majority of Christians, however, we are likely to encounter persecution "by more subtle means, by slander and lies." One only needs to peruse the world of "Catholic social media" for five minutes or listen in to the gossip in the church vestibule after Sunday Mass to see how true that statement is. Still, in societies where religion is derided or dismissed as superstitious or stupid, "persecution can take the form of gibes that try to caricature our faith and make us seem ridiculous" (GE 94). When, in striving to live the Gospel sincerely, we accept the bad that comes our way along with the good, that's what holiness looks like.

How True Holiness Will Be Judged

After dedicating the majority of this chapter to looking at the eight Beatitudes, Pope Francis returns to the larger picture of Christian holiness and how, particularly, we will be judged by God. Unsurprisingly, the pope points to the famous "criterion" for righteous living taught by Jesus in Matthew 25: "I was hungry and you gave me food, I was thirsty and you gave me drink, a stranger and you welcomed me, naked and you clothed me, ill and you cared for me, in prison and you visited me" (vv. 35-36). Notably, there's nothing in Jesus's words in that passage about adherence to specific doctrinal statements or an evaluation of what political party you support. It's about love of God through loving acts of mercy to one's neighbor.

Following St. John Paul II's teachings, Pope Francis reminds us that holiness is not just intellectual or "spiritual" in some disembodied sense, but it is practical and concrete. Using images like that of encountering a homeless person on a city street, the pope is calling us to always remember that what we say, what we do, and how we perceive one another and the world around us is how we arrive at Christian holiness. This happens at the local level, such as showing mercy to a homeless man, but it also happens at the structural level, especially when there are laws and cultures that threaten the lives and dignity of human persons and the whole creation. We are called to embrace what the late Cardinal Joseph Bernardin of Chicago called the "consistent ethic of life" or the "seamless garment" approach to Catholic ethics, recognizing the integral relationship of all threats to justice and peace.[10]

To this end, Pope Francis draws our attention to what he calls "ideologies" that get in the way of Christian holiness.

> What we say, what we do, and how we perceive one another and the world around us is how we arrive at Christian holiness.

On the one hand, he says there is a temptation to work for social justice while separating such important efforts from the Gospel and our relationship with the Lord. In this case, "Christianity thus becomes a sort of NGO stripped of the luminous mysticism so evident in the lives of St. Francis of Assisi, St. Vincent de Paul, St. Teresa of Calcutta, and many others" (GE 100). On the other hand, he says that the "other harmful ideological error is found in those who find suspect the social engagement of others, seeing it as superficial, worldly, secular, materialist, communist or populist" (GE 101). This latter group is common in the American context wherein we see certain Christians claim that the Gospel call for social justice is "Marxist" or something antithetical to real Christian holiness. The pope makes clear that such a claim is unfounded and that you cannot be holy without social engagement.

> You cannot be holy without social engagement.

Furthermore, this latter temptation also has a way of fostering the belief that Catholic Christians, in particular, ought to understand themselves as a "one issue" community. That issue for many in the American context is abortion. And while this is an important moral issue that the pope reiterates we need to be firm and passionate about, he adopts the longstanding tradition of a "consistent ethic of life" in stating that we cannot pick and choose our issues. "Equally sacred, however, are the lives of the poor, those already born, the destitute, the abandoned and the underprivileged, the vulnerable infirm and elderly exposed to covert euthanasia, the victims of human trafficking, new forms of slavery, and every form of rejection" (GE 101). Those who think that holiness consists of protecting the lives of the unborn at the expense of those already born miss the point of the Gospel, of Jesus's teachings, and of the entire tradition of God's revelation that dates back to the Old Testament (GE 103).

The pope concludes this chapter with a short section on prayer and worship, calling us to reconsider the way we think about what is pleasing to God. While, yes, prayer and celebrating the sacraments is important, Pope Francis explains that, "Our worship becomes pleasing to God when we devote ourselves to living generously, and allow God's gift, granted in prayer, to be shown in concern for our brothers and sisters" (GE 104). Going to Mass regularly, praying the Liturgy of the Hours or the rosary, attending holy hours, praying novenas or other devotionals do not mean much if they are not supported by the charitable acts of love we show to others, especially those most vulnerable and marginalized in our communities. As Pope Francis summarizes at the end of the chapter, "Christianity is meant above all to be put into practice" (GE 109).

Suggestions for Prayer

1. Pope Francis reminds us that our prayers mean nothing if they are not put into action. In the Gospel, Jesus's disciples ask him how to pray and he teaches them the Our Father in return. As we pray the common prayers we know so well, let us proclaim the words slowly and listen for the Spirit's voice speaking to us the teaching of Christ who reminds us that it is only when we do the will of God ("thy will be done") that the Kingdom of God begins to break into the world ("thy kingdom come . . . on earth as it is in heaven").

2. Which of the eight Beatitudes is the most challenging for you right now? Reflect in prayer on why that is and where God is calling you to grow in living the Gospel in your daily life.

Reflection Questions

1. Pope Francis spends a lot of time in this chapter highlighting the ways that Christian living, authentic discipleship, and true holiness do not align comfortably with the values of our world. Where do you see this disconnect between the teachings of Jesus and the messages of our contemporary society?

2. What are some of the "harmful ideologies" you see playing out in your local faith community? What are some of the ways you see the two temptations—justice without faith; faith without justice—appearing in your own life?

3. What does it look like for you to put your prayer and worship into action?

4 Signs of Holiness in Today's World

Pope Francis has always demonstrated his commitment to drawing from the rich tradition of the church, and the sources for his teaching in *Gaudete et Exsultate* are no exception to that rule. In the last chapter he focused on what the Second Vatican Council fathers would call *ressourcement* (a French word meaning "return to the sources") by examining Sacred Scripture and inviting us to recall the foundations of our faith in the life, ministry, and actions of Jesus Christ. In this chapter, Pope Francis again follows the lead of the Second Vatican Council by shifting his focus to *aggiornamento* (an Italian word meaning "bringing up to date") by examining five "spiritual attitudes" that are necessary for us to understand Christian holiness in the modern world. Together, these two chapters help form the complementary dynamic of going back to the tradition in order to move forward into the future. This process is beautifully illustrated by the West African Ghanaian expression *sankofa* (a Twi word meaning "go back and bring it"), which has been traditionally depicted in art as a bird facing forward to the future with its head turned back toward the past. In moving forward toward what is new and constructive, we must always be sure to take with us the tradition and sure-footedness of our collective past.

Pope Francis invites us to embrace these five expressions of love for God and neighbor in our journey of Christian holiness as an important response to contemporary cultures that are too often afflicted with anxiety, negativity, violence, distractions, consumerism, individualism, and superficial answers to profound spiritual questions (GE 111). In turn, let us look at these five themes and consider how we may incorporate them into our own journeys of faith.

1. Perseverance, Patience, and Meekness

In what or whom do you place your trust? What or who serves as your spiritual, psychological, or emotional anchor? It is these sorts of questions that motivate Pope Francis's first area of spiritual *aggiornamento*. Though he does not explicitly use the language of resilience, this gets at his primary aim. In an age when there is so much uncertainty and rapid change brought about by our digital world, it can be difficult to weather all that comes our way. Just as one's psychological, emotional, and physical experience can be affected by the instantaneousness of our news cycle and means of communication—*can we ever get away from the news?*—so too our spiritual lives are affected. While elsewhere the pope has celebrated the technological advancements that make such communication possible he, like his predecessor Benedict XVI, is concerned about the shadow side of these media as well. And it is this that particularly worries Pope Francis when he reflects on what it means for a modern woman or man who wishes to pursue the path of Christian holiness.

As we saw in chapter 2, the internet and social media landscape can be a vile and treacherous place. A Christian who takes his or her baptismal call seriously will "need to recognize and combat our aggressive and selfish inclinations, and not let them take root" (GE 114). This is especially challenging when social media trolls or anonymous commenters who appear to enjoy stirring the proverbial pot to get an angry rise out of readers bombard us with their vitriol. But, sadly, this sort of behavior and attitude is coming not only from outside the Christian community. "Christians too can be caught up in the networks of verbal violence through the Internet and the various forums of digital communication. Even in Catholic media, limits can be overstepped, defamation and slander can become commonplace, and all ethical standards and respect for the good name of others can be abandoned" (GE 115).

This is where patience and meekness come in. We will be faced with circumstances and environments that challenge our ability to truly live a Christian life of holiness, temptations that invite a violent response to others in word and deed. The pope says that it is only "inner strength, as the work of grace, [that] prevents us from becoming carried away by the violence that is so much a part of life today" (GE 116). While this grace is always freely offered to us, it is our cooperation with God's gift that allows us to live a life of holiness. We must practice being patient and learn to embrace a disposition of meekness. In a strikingly modern footnote in this section, Pope Francis names bullying as something that commonly causes great harm to others, especially to one's sense of self and self-esteem. This bullying, he adds, can take on something of a passive-aggressive form that presents itself as "seemingly delicate or respectful and even quite spiritual" but really only brings other people down (GE 117 n. 95). How we respond to those circumstances in which we find ourselves the target of such humiliations will reveal much about where we stand on our journey toward holiness.

2. Joy and Sense of Humor

Early in Pope Francis's earlier apostolic exhortation, *Evangelii Gaudium*, there appears the memorable line: "There are Christians

> It is our cooperation with God's gift that allows us to live a life of holiness.

whose lives seem like Lent without Easter" (EG 6). Here he is calling to task those Christians who interpret the seriousness of the Gospel as demanding an attitude and appearance of a humorless buzzkill. One of the most consistent themes of Pope Francis's ministry as Bishop of Rome has been to highlight the joy that comes with choosing to follow Jesus Christ, which is why he reiterates in *Gaudete et Exsultate*: "Far from being timid, morose, acerbic or melancholy, or putting on a dreary face, the saints are joyful and full of good humor" (GE 122). Too often we mistake somberness or dreariness for realism and seriousness in the Christian life. Pope Francis is making clear the point that his fellow Jesuit Father James Martin articulated well in the introduction of his book *Between Heaven and Mirth: Why Joy, Humor, and Laughter Are at the Heart of the Spiritual Life*. Fr. Martin writes that a lighthearted spirit "is an essential element of a healthy spiritual life and a healthy life in general. When we lose sight of this serious truth, we cease to live life fully, truly, and wholly."[1] Joy and humor, lightheartedness and peace are hallmarks of the Christian life. Pope Francis provides a list of scriptural examples in which the holy ones of faith have exhibited joy, happiness, and exhilaration: the prophets, Mary the mother of God, and Jesus, to name a few, bear witness to the place of the lighthearted spirit in the spiritual life.

To be a serious Christian *does not mean* taking oneself too seriously. It means taking the message of Jesus Christ and the lived witness of faith with utmost importance, but that includes a presence in the world that is easily recognized as joyful and welcoming. Taking oneself too seriously and acting with self-importance disguised as superficial holiness is really a kind of self-preoccupation and self-centeredness, which seeks to communicate to others "I am better than you, more special than you, more serious about my faith than you, more holy than you!" Pope Francis has frequently pointed out that this is no way to live the

Christian faith. In fact, if one actually accepts the Lord's invitation and delights in the relationship of love that God extends to us, we are changed by that encounter and rejoice in that love. Earlier in this document, Pope Francis has said: "Thanks solely to this encounter—or renewed encounter—with God's love, which blossoms into an enriching friendship, we are liberated from our narrowness and self-absorption. We become fully human when we are more than human, when we let God bring us beyond ourselves in order to attain the fullest truth of our being" (GE 8).

As Scripture scholars have noted for some time, Jesus had a good sense of humor. Because we have become so accustomed to hearing the stories of the Gospel over and over again, and we live in an era and culture admittedly different from Jesus's own, we do not often appreciate the humor with which Jesus preached and taught. Pope Francis wants us to know that to be holy does not mean surrendering the ability to laugh or tell a good joke or enjoy good company. In fact, this is part of what is attractive about the Christian life to others. Holy women and men draw others to themselves, not because there is anything particularly special about them, but because in rejoicing in the love of God they can be glad—and this joy captures the attention of others.

3. Boldness and Passion

Pope Francis introduces a Greek word that is likely unfamiliar to most people: *parrhesía*. Here the pope uses it to describe "boldness," but in its ancient context it was used more specifically to describe prophetic speech. In this way we can see why the Holy Father chose this term and explains that another sign of holiness in the modern world is exhibited by "an impulse to evangelize and to

> To be holy does not mean surrendering the ability to laugh or tell a good joke or enjoy good company.

leave a mark in this world" (GE 129). Fear inhibits us from act-ing with the convictions we profess to believe. Fear prevents us from being bold in our faith and courageous with our words and deeds. And yet, boldness in working for justice and peace, rec-onciliation and communion, is a hallmark of Christian holiness.

When we examine the lives of the saints, we see time and again boldness in word and deed that signals their sanctity and clear response to their baptismal call. One thinks, for example, of St. Maximilian Kolbe, who with boldness and immedi-acy volunteered his own life to save that of a young father while imprisoned in the Auschwitz concentration camp during World War II. Or one thinks of the great martyrs of the early church, St. Perpetua and St. Felicity, who boldly bore wit-ness to their faith in Christ despite the threat to their lives and their eventual murder for the sake of the faith. Or one thinks of the bold preaching of St. Óscar Romero, St. Catherine of Siena, and so many others who heeded Jesus's words, "Do not be afraid," in order to proclaim Jesus Christ and denounce structures of injustice and abuse in their midst.

Pope Francis calls our attention once again to the example of Jesus. "His deep compassion reached out to others. It did not make him hesitant, timid or self-conscious, as often happens with us. Quite the opposite. His compassion made him go out actively to preach and to send others on a mission of healing and liberation" (GE 131). Holiness is not a matter of staying isolated, sheltered, or protected in the communities and spaces we feel most comfortable. Many people today—perhaps some of those who also reject the joy and humor constitutive of holiness—have a mistaken and distorted sense that Christian holiness is achieved only when one embraces a spirit of *fuga mundi*, an ancient Latin expression that means "to flee the world." It's notable that Jesus

> Boldness in working for justice and peace, reconciliation and communion, is a hallmark of Christian holiness.

never tells his disciples to leave the world. In fact, in the Gospel of John, Jesus prays to the Father that his followers might be sent *into the world* but that they *not be of the world* (John 17:6-26). We are called to go boldly into the world to proclaim Jesus Christ in word and deed, not shy away from the world and the challenges before us.

The risk we face in not being bold in our witness is that we become complacent. This is true personally and collectively, which is why the pope challenges the church to "not stand still, but constantly welcome the Lord's surprises" (GE 139). It's very tempting to maintain the status quo. "Complacency is seductive; it tells us that there is no point in trying to change things, that there is nothing we can do, because this is the way things have always been and yet we always manage to survive" (GE 137). You cannot be holy and go through the motions, resigned to let things unfold in whatever which way because you are unwilling or afraid. "God is not afraid!" Pope Francis says, "He is fearless! He is always greater than our plans and schemes. Unafraid of the fringes, he himself became a fringe (cf. Philippians 2:6-8; John 1:14). So if we dare to go to the fringes, we will find him there; indeed, he is already there. Jesus is already there, in the hearts of our brothers and sisters, in their wounded flesh, in their troubles and in their profound desolation" (GE 135). Christ calls us to go boldly to the margins—the fringes—of our society because that is where Christ is found. God came into this world as one of us to show us both who God is and who we are called to be (John 1:18). The only way we can pursue holiness is to do what he has shown and told us to do.

4. Community

Christ calls us to go boldly to the margins.

As with the themes of mercy and joy, another touchstone of Pope Francis's teaching is the centrality of community in Christian life. If community were not so key to God's vision for the Kingdom, then Jesus would never have called together disciples, Jesus would never have healed those marginalized by their illnesses so as to allow them to return to community, Jesus would never have taught in parables the prioritized interdependence and relationship, and Jesus would have appeared only to individuals after the resurrection instead of when two or more were gathered. God's intention for us is to live in community, and our journey of faith can take place only within that collective effort. "Growth in holiness is a journey in community, side by side with others" (GE 141).

This begins in baptism, when each of us was incorporated into the Body of Christ, which is the church. This bond joins all of us together no matter where we find ourselves in the world, which is why the Second Vatican Council could confidently proclaim: "All the faithful, scattered though they be throughout the world, are in communion with each other in the Holy Spirit."[2] So powerful is this bond of community that it extends beyond time and space to include all those who have been or will also be baptized into Christ's Body, a tenet of our faith that we call "the communion of saints." If we cannot live our faith as Christians alone but only in community, why would we ever think that we could pursue a life of holiness independently?

Not only do individuals seek holiness within the community, aided along the way by their sisters and brothers, but Pope Francis also notes that at times entire local communities can attain holiness together. He offers by way of example several historical instances in which whole groups have been martyred or otherwise exhibited a sense of Christian love and hospitality. Among those communities, he names the Trappist Monks of Tibhirine, Algeria, who collectively bore witness to Christian peace, interreligious dialogue, and fraternal love for their neighbors—Christian and non-Christian alike. They were kidnapped and murdered by an armed terrorist group in 1996, and their story has been memorialized in the powerful 2010 film *Of Gods and Men*.[3]

It's not only professed women and men in consecrated life that can strive for Christian holiness together. Pope Francis also points to the local community of the family, which has often been described in Catholic teaching as "the domestic church." Building on his earlier teaching in the apostolic exhortation on love and the family, *Amoris Laetitia*, the pope says: "In many holy marriages, too, each spouse becomes a means used by Christ for the sanctification of the other" (GE 141). This again sheds light on an important if often overlooked truth of the faith: holiness is not achieved by grand mystical or heroic experiences, but in the small, everyday, common activities and decisions of life. To illustrate this point, Pope Francis calls our focus to Jesus's own manner of paying attention to the seemingly unimportant and little details:

> At times entire local communities can attain holiness together.

> The little detail that wine was running out at a party.
> The little detail that one sheep was missing.
> The little detail of noticing the widow who offered her two small coins.
> The little detail of having spare oil for the lamps, should the bridegroom delay.
> The little detail of asking the disciples how many loaves of bread they had.
> The little detail of having a fire burning and a fish cooking as he waited for the disciples at daybreak. (GE 144)

It is indeed God's intention that we live together as one (John 17:21), but that is not accomplished with over-the-top gestures and actions; the process of living together in holiness is one of attention to the little things, the details of life that challenge us to love and serve one another.

> The process of living together in holiness is one of attention to the little things.

5. Constant Prayer

The last section of this chapter focuses on prayer. It may seem an obvious topic to address in an apostolic exhortation on holiness, but, if we're being honest, most of us struggle to be consistent in our prayer. Pope Francis calls us not only to be consistent, like going to Mass weekly, but rather *constant* in prayer. This may seem daunting, but it is something that we practice and develop. One model of what it looks like to become someone who is constant in prayer is the pope's namesake, St. Francis of Assisi. One of his earliest biographers noted that it took a long time for St. Francis to live in such a way that his intention to follow the Gospel more seriously was evident in his thoughts and actions. He was described as being committed to following Christ "in mind" but not yet "in action." Only over time did St. Francis realize that everything he did, thought, and said was a form of communication with God because, as St. Augustine famously said, God is the one closer to us than we are to ourselves.[4] Recognizing that prayer is communication with God, St. Francis slowly was able to more greatly attune his heart and mind to God at all times. In this way, St. Francis moved from merely "saying prayers" to over time becoming "a living prayer."[5]

How do we become a living prayer? Is this only something for a select number of special people? Pope Francis says that, because all the baptized share this universal call to holiness, "I would insist that this is true not only for a privileged few, but for all of us" (GE 149). Holiness is impossible without prayer and holiness is not something that we can pursue in a compartmentalized way. Therefore, any sense of authentic Christian holiness will entail a shift in our thinking that encourages us to integrate prayer—a sense of constant communication to God by our deeds, words, and thoughts—into the whole fabric of our lives. One way to help us along this path is to regularly return to Scripture, which beckons us to imagine ourselves in the story of God's revelation and hear the Spirit's call in the sacred Word of God.

Of course, there are special ways to pray along the journey of our lives. Pope Francis encourages us to adopt certain practices to help us along the path toward becoming people who pray constantly. One of the most significant forms of prayer we are invited to prioritize is intercessory prayer—that is, praying for the needs of others. "Prayer of intercession has particular value, for it is an act of trust in God and, at the same time, an expression of love for our neighbor" (GE 154). As Pope Francis says, intercessory prayer allows us to reconnect with God, seeking assistance or offering gratitude on behalf of others, which itself is a service to our sisters and brothers. It is a relatively easy spiritual practice, too. How simple it is to say to somebody we know or have met, "I will pray for you," and then bring that intercession before God when we next pause to focus our attention on our Creator. The difficulty is, however, setting aside the time to do precisely that. This discipline of making time to be alone with God, to bring our needs and those of others before God, is how we develop the habit of prayer that can transform us from people who occasionally pray to those who pray constantly with our whole lives.

How do we become a living prayer?

Suggestions for Prayer

1. Set aside a little time each day during which you will leave behind all distractions (cell phones and other technology included) just to be quiet in the presence of God. Bring before God your life, all those things for which you are grateful and those things that are causing stress, anxiety,

or sadness. Also, present the needs and prayers of those for whom you have promised to pray.

2. Reflect on what it might be like for your life to become a "living prayer" in the spirit of St. Francis and the teachings of Pope Francis. Are you aware of the ways your thoughts, words, decisions, and actions communicate something to God? What exactly *are you communicating* to God?

Reflection Questions

1. In what ways do you find the need for perseverance, patience, and meekness in your own Christian journey? What are the challenges you face in being resilient in today's world?

2. What place do joy and humor play in your own faith experience? Have you had experiences—of yourself or others—where someone takes themselves too seriously all in the name of being a "good Christian"? What did that attitude communicate about the faith?

3. What are the biggest challenges and blessings for you about community as the place where one encounters authentic Christian holiness?

5 Spiritual Combat, Vigilance, and Discernment

The final chapter of *Gaudete et Exsultate* takes a turn that many modern readers might find unexpected. Pope Francis introduces the notion that the "Christian life is a constant battle" (GE 158). To some people, this language will remind them of devotional prayers and narratives of generations past (think of the prayer to St. Michael the Archangel who "defends us in battle" against "wickedness and snares of the devil"). To others, this language could be alienating or confusing ("Isn't Christianity about love, justice, and peace? What's with the battle language?"). In the spirit of the Second Vatican Council's pattern of both *ressourcement* and *aggiornamento* discussed at the outset of the last chapter, the pope here is drawing from a classic spiritual metaphor for the Christian struggle—"battle" against the devil—but does not merely repeat outdated and theologically inadequate views of ages past. Instead, he takes the metaphor and develops it for our time.

Setting the stage for a richer understanding of this language, Pope Francis explains the parameters of this "battle." He notes that it is, on the one hand, a matter of resisting the "worldly mentality that would deceive us and leave us dull and mediocre, lacking in enthusiasm and joy" and combating our own personal human weaknesses and challenges (e.g., laziness, lust, envy, etc.).

And, on the other hand, "it is also a constant struggle against the devil, the prince of evil" (GE 159).

Those who have followed Pope Francis's weekday homilies and other addresses closely will not be surprised at his mention of the devil. As theologian Gregory Hillis explains, "A search on the Vatican website reveals that so far during his tenure, Pope Francis has mentioned the devil as often as Pope St. John Paul II and Pope Benedict XVI combined."[1] Few people, even people of faith, feel comfortable talking about "the devil" or "Satan" in polite conversation. To many, such language seems mythical and surreal, a vestige of an earlier time when science and medicine had not been invented to explain the apparent supernatural experience of the world in which we live. Pope Francis acknowledges that there are certainly cases in which the biblical authors "had limited conceptual resources for expressing certain realities" that we might today attribute to psychology, biology, and natural occurrences (GE 160). And yet, the pope is adamant about reminding Christians that we believe we are, as theologians are fond of saying, "more than the sum of our parts." We recognize and profess belief in a spiritual reality that cannot be entirely accessed, assessed, and understood by empirical investigation. Science cannot make sense of the incarnation or the communion of saints or so many aspects of our faith. And so while science and human discovery have helped and continue to help us make sense of our world and ourselves, "this should not lead us to an oversimplification that would conclude that all cases related in the Gospel had to do with psychological disorders and hence that the devil does not exist or is not at work" (GE 160).

To make this point even clearer, Pope Francis says: "we should not think of the devil as a myth, a symbol, a figure of speech or an idea" (GE 161). The pope teaches that when we dismiss the reality of evil in general or the devil in particular, we fall prey to a tactic the devil uses to throw us off guard and make us vulnerable. As Pope Francis stated in a 2014 homily, "The devil exists in the twenty-first century. We mustn't be naïve. We must learn from the Gospel how to fight against him."[2] This is the spiritual combat—the battle—about which Pope Francis is speaking. How do we resist this tempter who, as the First Letter of Peter reminds us, is "prowling around like a roaring lion looking for [someone] to devour" (5:8)?

In his analysis of Pope Francis's preaching and teaching on the theme of evil and the devil, Hillis explains: "The pope argues that the devil, knowing unity rooted in love characterizes the church, seeks to destroy the church through division."[3] Division is the devil's modus operandi, it is the tool he uses to discourage Christians in their faith, break up communities of believers, turn the faithful—including religious leaders—against one another, and disrupt all effort to bring about the Kingdom of God. Pope Francis speaks often about the "terrorism of gossip," that malicious practice that creeps into otherwise ordinary and innocent conversation when we find ourselves choosing to share something unflattering or salacious about another person. This is just one of the many ways the devil works to throw us off the path of Christian holiness, which is why St. Paul was so insistent that Christians "build one another up" rather than tear one another down (Rom 14:19).

In naming the devil and spiritual combat at the end of this exhortation, the pope is making clear that the path to Christian holiness is not a one-time, singular experience but instead a lifelong "battle" against the barrage of temptations that confront us. The only way we can continue on this ongoing journey toward holiness is by counting on the "weapons" of prayer that God has bestowed on us, especially the sacraments. But it is not enough merely to go to Mass. We are called, as we saw in the last chapter, to become people whose whole lives become a prayer. Can we transform ourselves into people whose hearts and minds are focused on God in all that we think, say, or do? Can we draw on the Word of God for guidance and wisdom, build one another up in the spirit of community life, and reach out to those at the margins of our societies as the missionary disciples Christ has called us and Pope Francis has reminded us to be? "Along this journey, the cultivation of all that is good, progress in the spiritual life and growth in love are the best counterbalance to evil" (GE 162).

This brings Pope Francis to the theme of vigilance. In a sense, this theme has hovered over much of his reflection on Christian holiness. The key here is to be awake and ready, not just "going through the motions" as we often say. This is seen in numerous passages of the Gospel when Jesus calls for precisely this attention on the part of his followers (see Luke 12:35; Matt 24:42; Mark 13:35). The theme of vigilance in the life of discipleship appears in the pope's near-constant refrain for us to avoid dulling our consciences by succumbing to the distractions and complacency the world places before us. "Those who think they commit no grievous sins against God's law can fall into a state of dull lethargy" (GE 164). Indeed, most of us convince ourselves that we are decent people, who generally do good things and care about others. And while that may be true, there is a reason each time we gather for Eucharist that we acknowledge not only the sins we have committed but also "in what we have failed to do." The person lukewarm in her faith, the person whose conscience is dull and indifferent—these are the people who veer off the path of holiness. Pope Francis sees this as perhaps even worse than a dramatic sinful break: "Spiritual corruption is worse than the fall of a sinner, for it is a comfortable and self-satisfied form of blindness" (GE 165).

The final theme that Pope Francis addresses in this chapter is that of discernment. As a Jesuit, the pope was trained in a spiritual tradition founded by St. Ignatius Loyola that prioritized discernment in the spiritual life. The Holy Father brings the gift of this tradition to the broader church near the end of his exhortation, explaining that dedication to prayer and discernment is how we come to understand what is from God and what is from the world or, worse, the devil (GE 166). Discernment is something more than book learning or even street knowledge. Discernment is a fruit of our vigilance and openness to the Spirit's work in our lives. Naming the rapid changes of the world in which we live, the pope recognizes that discernment is all the more important today. He says that there is a twofold tendency for people to fall into a trap in the face of novelty. At times, God is calling us to change and develop, but we resist it and use our faith as an excuse to maintain the status quo. Other times, it is the world or even the devil that plants the idea that something has to give, and we embrace it blindly. Both cases are instances in which discernment is not present. Anyone who has had to make a major decision about family or career knows the difficulty of determining what God is calling for in that case. If we don't practice following the Lord faithfully, opening ourselves to the inspiration of the Holy Spirit, and remaining vigilant in a rapidly changing world, then not only our major but also our daily, minor decisions will seem insurmountable. Practice is the key; practice the discipline of prayerful discernment! Referring to the wisdom of St. Ignatius, the pope recounts that "often discernment is exercised in small and apparently irrelevant things, since greatness of spirit is manifested in simple everyday realities" (GE 169).

One thing that Pope Francis asks us to avoid is magical thinking. Discernment is not some process by which God literally speaks to us the course we should pursue or the decision that we ought to make. We must take into consideration other factors as well, but "we should always remember that discernment is

> Discernment is a fruit of our vigilance and openness to the Spirit's work in our lives.

a grace. Even though it includes reason and prudence, it goes beyond them, for it seeks a glimpse of that unique and mysterious plan that God has for each of us, which takes shape amid so many situations and limitations" (GE 170). Pope Francis talks about the product of discernment as "a new synthesis that springs from a life inspired by the Spirit" (GE 171). In this way we can think of our discernment as a means of cooperating with God rather than going it on our own or expecting God to dictate concrete instructions to us.

In the end, the meaning of Christian holiness rests in the willingness of each member of the faithful to embrace the call that they received at baptism. We are destined to be saints, like the many women and men who have lived our way of life and have gone before us. But this is very much a choice: a choice between authentic holiness and "false forms of holiness"; a choice between embracing the Beatitudes or rejecting them; a choice between living out the signs of holiness in today's world or going our own way; a choice between resisting temptation and the devil or discerning, with the help of the Spirit and others we love and trust, the path God has laid before us.

At the opening of this apostolic exhortation, Pope Francis made it clear that what followed was not an academic presentation about holiness in some abstract sense, "containing definitions and distinctions" about what sanctification means. Instead, he sought to "repropose the call to holiness in a practical way for our time, with all its risks, challenges, and opportunities" (GE 2). It is my hope that this guide has aided in that noble and timely effort and encouraged you to return often to *Gaudete et Exsultate* for inspiration, challenge, and guidance in your journey toward Christian holiness as disciples walking in the footsteps of Jesus Christ.

Suggestions for Prayer

1. Reflect on the ways you recognize (or do not see) evil operating in the world around you and in your own life. Pray for the assistance of the Holy Spirit in resisting the temptations that come from the "prince of evil" and the openness to respond to God's call in your life.

2. Think of some decision—big or small—that you are facing right now in your life. Bring that matter to prayer and seek the gift of discernment necessary to make the choice that cooperates best with God.

Reflection Questions

1. Every Easter we renew our baptismal promises, during which we profess to "Reject Satan and all his empty promises," yet few people are willing to discuss or even acknowledge the existence of the devil in our world. Where do you stand on this matter of faith? How do you understand the devil's place in the world and in our faith?

2. Following the teaching of Jesus Christ, Pope Francis calls us to be vigilant and awake. How might you grow in your vigilance as a person of faith on the path to holiness? What are some of the stumbling blocks or challenges for you?

3. Where do you see the Spirit speaking to you in your discernment? Through a parish minister or spiritual director? Through a close friend or family member? Through your reading of Sacred Scripture? How can you improve your openness to the Spirit's call in your own life?

Notes

Introduction

1. Thomas Merton, *The Seven Storey Mountain* (New York: Harcourt Brace, 1998), 260–61.

2. James Martin, "Don't Call Me A Saint?," *America* (November 14, 2012).

3. For an excellent and accessible overview of the levels of teaching authority, see Richard R. Gaillardetz, *By What Authority? Foundations for Understanding Authority in the Church*, 2nd ed. (Collegeville, MN: Liturgical Press, 2018).

4. All of the documents of the Second Vatican Council referenced in this book are available online in multiple languages at: http://www.vatican.va/archive/hist_councils/ii_vatican_council/index.htm.

5. Gaillardetz, *By What Authority?*, 171–73.

Chapter 1

1. See Elizabeth A. Johnson, *Friends of God and Prophets: A Feminist Theological Reading of the Communion of Saints* (New York: Continuum, 1999); and Benedict XVI, "Homily for the Solemn Inauguration of the Petrine Ministry" (April 24, 2005), AAS 97 (2005): 708.

2. The reference to *Lumen Gentium* comes from paragraph 9.

3. "Mother Teresa: 'Do Small Things with Great Love,'" *Catholic News Service* (September 4, 2016). Available at http://www.catholicnews.com/services/englishnews/2016/mother-teresa-do-small-things-with-great-love.cfm.

4. Thomas of Celano, "The Remembrance of the Desire of a Soul," bk. 2, no. 214, in *Francis of Assisi: Early Documents*, ed. Regis J. Armstrong, J. A. Wayne Hellmann, and William J. Short, vol. 2 (New York: New City Press, 2000), 386.

5. The original reference comes from the New Zealand Catholic Bishops' Conference, *Healing Love* (January 1, 1988).

6. See Thomas Merton, *New Seeds of Contemplation* (New York: New Directions Publishing, 1961).

Chapter 2

1. *Catholic News Service*, "Vatican PR Aide Warns Catholic Blogs Create 'Cesspool of Hatred,'" (May 17, 2016). Available at https://cruxnow.com /cns/2016/05/17/vatican-pr-aide-warns-catholic-blogs-create-cesspool -of-hatred/.

2. Bonaventure, *Itinerarium Mentis in Deum*, bk. 7, chap. 5, ed. Philotheus Boehner and Zachary Hayes, Works of St. Bonaventure 2 (St. Bonaventure: Franciscan Institute Publications, 2002), 137.

3. Antonio Spadaro, "A Big Heart Open to God: An Interview with Pope Francis," *America Magazine* (September 30, 2013). Available at https://www.americamagazine.org/faith/2013/09/30/big-heart -open-god-interview-pope-francis.

4. Spadaro, "A Big Heart Open to God."

5. Francis of Assisi, "A Letter to Brother Anthony of Padua," no. 2, in *Francis of Assisi: Early Documents*, ed. Regis J. Armstrong, J. A. Wayne Hellmann, and William J. Short, vol. 1 (New York: New City Press, 1999), 107.

6. Francis of Assisi, "The Later Rule (1223)," chap. 5, no. 2, in *Francis of Assisi: Early Documents*, vol. 1, 102.

7. *The Roman Missal*, 3rd typical edition (Collegeville, MN: Liturgical Press, 2011), 616.

8. *Catechism of the Catholic Church*, 2nd ed. (United States Catholic Conference—Libreria Editrice Vaticana, 1997).

9. This document is available online at http://www.vatican.va/roman_curia /pontifical_councils/chrstuni/documents/rc_pc_chrstuni_doc_31101999 _cath-luth-joint-declaration_en.html.

10. Francis of Assisi, "Admonition V," nos. 4–8, in *Francis of Assisi: Early Documents*, vol. 1, 131.

Chapter 3

1. This terminology is recounted, for example, in the Acts of the Apostles at the calling of Saul, who was known to persecute those who were "following the Way" (Acts 9:2). For more, see Luke Timothy Johnson, *The Acts of the Apostles*, Sacra Pagina 5 (Collegeville, MN: Liturgical Press, 1992), 161–62.

2. Kyle Scott Clauss, "The Millennium Tower's $37.5 Million Penthouse Has a Buyer," *Boston Magazine* (February 11, 2016). Available at https://www.bostonmagazine.com/news/2016/02/11/millennium -tower-penthouse-sold/.

3. Lawrence Holben, *All the Way to Heaven: A Theological Reflection on Dorothy Day, Peter Maurin, and the Catholic Worker* (Eugene, OR: Wipf and Stock, 1997), 34.

4. Pope Francis, "Homily for the Mass for the Possession of the Chair of the Bishop of Rome" (April 7, 2013), in *The Church of Mercy: A Vision for the Church* (Chicago: Loyola Press, 2014), 3.

5. Pope Francis, *Misericordiae Vultus*, no. 6 (April 11, 2015). Available at https://w2.vatican.va/content/francesco/en/apost_letters/documents/papa -francesco_bolla_20150411_misericordiae-vultus.html.

6. Pope Francis, *Misericordiae Vultus*, no. 9.

7. Francis of Assisi, "Canticle of the Creatures," no. 10, in *Francis of Assisi: Early Documents*, vol. 1, 114.

8. Óscar Romero, *The Violence of Love*, trans. James R. Brockman (Maryknoll, NY: Orbis Books, 2004), 16.

9. Romero, *The Violence of Love*, 142.

10. For more on this, see Joseph Cardinal Bernardin, *Consistent Ethic of Life*, ed. Thomas G. Fuechtmann (Lanham, MD: Rowman & Littlefield, 1988).

Chapter 4

1. James Martin, *Between Heaven and Mirth: Why Joy, Humor, and Laughter Are at the Heart of the Spiritual Life* (San Francisco: HarperOne, 2011), 2.

2. Vatican II, *Lumen Gentium*, no. 13.

3. The original French film is titled *Des Hommes et des Dieux*, directed by Xavier Beauvois (2010).

4. See Augustine, *Confessions*, 3.6.11, trans. Henry Chadwick (New York: Oxford University Press, 1998), 43.

5. See Thomas of Celano, "The First Life of Francis of Assisi," bk. 2, chap. 4, no. 97, in *Francis of Assisi: Early Documents*, vol. 1, 266. Also, see Daniel P. Horan, "Prayer in the Franciscan Tradition," in *Prayer in the Catholic Tradition: A Handbook of Practical Approaches*, ed. Robert J. Wicks (Cincinnati: Franciscan Media, 2016), 177–208.

Chapter 5

1. Gregory K. Hillis, "Satan," in *A Pope Francis Lexicon*, ed. Joshua J. McElwee and Cindy Wooden (Collegeville, MN: Liturgical Press, 2018), 167.

2. April 2014 homily quoted in Hillis, "Satan," 168.

3. Hillis, "Satan," 169.

For Further Reading

Day, Dorothy. *Dorothy Day: Selected Writings*. Edited by Robert Ellsberg. Maryknoll, NY: Orbis Books, 1992.

Flanagan, Brian P. *Stumbling in Holiness: Sin and Sanctity in the Church*. Collegeville, MN: Liturgical Press, 2018.

Francis. *Amoris Laetitia*, The Joy of Love (March 19, 2016).

———. *Evangelii Gaudium*, The Joy of the Gospel (November 24, 2013).

———. *Laudato Sí*, On Care for Our Common Home (May 24, 2015).

Horan, Daniel P. *Dating God: Live and Love in the Way of St. Francis*. Cincinnati: Franciscan Media, 2012.

Johnson, Elizabeth A. *Friends of God and Prophets: A Feminist Theological Reading of the Communion of Saints*. New York: Continuum, 1999.

Merton, Thomas. *New Seeds of Contemplation*. New York: New Directions Publishing, 1961.

Romero, Óscar. *The Violence of Love*. Edited by James R. Brockman. Maryknoll, NY: Orbis Books, 2004.

Spadaro, Antonio. *A Big Heart Open to God: A Conversation with Pope Francis*. San Francisco: HarperOne, 2013.

Wicks, Robert J., ed. *Prayer in the Catholic Tradition: A Handbook of Practical Approaches*. Cincinnati: Franciscan Media, 2016.